WALLEYE
ACROSS CANADA

Henry Waszczuk 🍁 *Italo Labignan*

ISBN 0-9692391-2-2

1987 Canadian Sportfishing Productions
P.O. Box 84, Carlisle, Ontario
L0R 1H0

Copyright® **1987**

Dedication

It is with sincere love and appreciation that we dedicate this book to our families. Their encouragement and support has complimented our hectic lives both on and off the water.

Rhonda Labignan
Patricia
Jessica
John
Amanda

Mary Waszczuk
Jessica
Michael

Foreword

Fishing at its best is often a team sport. It seems sharing the great outdoors with a partner makes it even more enjoyable, whether that partner is a son or daughter, a wife or husband, or some other fishing buddy.

In "Walleye Across Canada", Italo Labignan and Henry Waszczuk have carried teamwork even further. Individually, each of these dedicated anglers is a true expert; together, they are even better.

"Walleye Across Canada" is written in such a way that it should make better walleye fishermen out of just about everyone, whether they are seasoned anglers or frustrated rookies.

Enjoy this fine book, learn from it, but remember that you don't have to keep your limit to have a good time. Release the fish that haven't been damaged or handled in the gills, and we should all enjoy good fishing for years to come.

Yours in Conservation,

R.G. Morgan
Executive Vice President
Ontario Federation of Anglers and Hunters

About the Authors

Both Henry Waszczuk and Italo Labignan are identified as Canada's most versatile fishing experts. Well-known as sportfishing personalities, writers, fishing educators, their busy schedule includes starring in their own "Canadian Sportfishing" TV series, seen nationwide on TSN – The Sports Network.

Besides writing hundreds of articles for major magazines, Henry and Italo make time each year to reach Canadian audiences with the newest in fishing techniques and products at major sportfishing expositions.

Thousands of people annually attend one of Canada's largest travelling sportfishing shows, their own "All Ontario Canadian Sportfishing Show."

Both of these fishing pros have fished for walleye under variety of conditions in all seasons nationwide. With their insight, knowledge and expertise, they have written the most comprehensive book on walleye fishing in Canada

Table of Contents
INTRODUCTION
CHAPTER 1 – THE FISH

CHAPTER 2 – HABITAT
Southern lakes (Eutrophic):

Northern lakes (Mezo-Oligotrophic):

CHAPTER 3 – FISHING PATTERNS
Southern lakes:

Northern lakes:

Small rivers:

Large rivers:

CHAPTER 4 – FISHING EQUIPMENT

CHAPTER 5 – ELECTRONIC EQUIPMENT

CHAPTER 6 – ARTIFICIAL LURES

CHAPTER 7 - LIVE BAIT

CHAPTER 8 - BOATS

CHAPTER 9 - COMPETITIVE WALLEYE FISHING

CHAPTER 10 - COMMON WALLEYE PARASITES, DISEASES & CONTAMINANTS

CHAPTER 11 - CLEANING & COOKING WALLEYE

CHAPTER 12 - CONSERVATION

GLOSSARY

Introduction

To many people this freshwater game fish is still commonly called a "yellow pickerel". Officially the fish that was known as the yellow pickerel is now called the "walleye". This name is more appropriate because it provides a better classification for this game fish. For years many people were confusing the smaller members of the pike family referred to as pickerel with the walleye, which they called "yellow pickerel." Therefore, the only time Canadians heard the term "walleye" would be when an American was talking about this popular fish. Now the name "walleye" will be common place. The term "walleye" refers to the smokey, opaque eye which is characteristic of this fish. In Quebec they are known as "Dore" because of their bright golden color.

Walleye

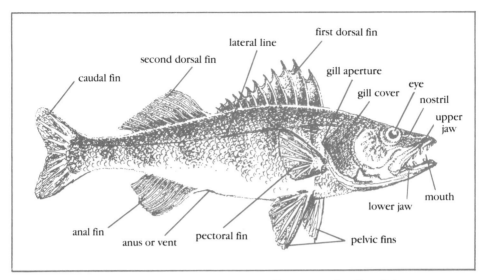

The walleye is the most sought after game fish by sport fishermen in Canada's inland waters . It is also a commercially sought after game fish in Ontario and some Prairie Provinces. Even though they are relatively easy to catch, walleye don't jump or fight magnificently when hooked. They usually splash furiously when you bring them to the surface and near the net. As a meal-time offering they are unsurpassed. The fish eating connoisseur need not worry about cleaning small bones, since filleting these fish is an easy task. The flesh of the walleye is white when cooked and has a mild fish flavour, that is enjoyed by hundreds of thousands of people annually.

The walleye is one of the largest members of the perch family and it can grow to weights of 30 lbs. In Canada, the average size of these fish is two to three pounds, with eight to ten pounders being considered trophies. Walleye fishing can be enjoyed both in the winter and in the summer. Since

walleye are schooling fish, once located they are quite easy to catch. When most fishermen catch one or two fish they often work that particular area and catch a limit. The common names for walleye are: pickerel, yellow pickerel, blue pickerel, jack, jack-fish, pike-perch and of course the most universally used - walleye!

Sauger

Some anglers are not aware that the walleye has a smaller cousin known as the "sauger". Few anglers are familiar with the sauger. The walleye and sauger appear similar in shape and configuration. The only prominent differences between the sauger and the walleye are listed below:

1) The sauger lacks the black patch located on the base of the first dorsal fin.

2) Saugers lack the milky-white patch on the lower part of the tail.

3) Prominent mottling can be seen on the sides of the sauger and there is spotting on the fins.

Saugers can be caught from Alberta, east to the St. Lawrence River in Quebec and north to the top of James Bay. The average length of Canadian saugers is ten to sixteen inches and their average weight is approximately one pound.

The sauger is an important sport and commercial fish in Canada. In Manitoba it is third in importance behind the walleye and whitefish. At one time saugers were harvested annually from the Great Lakes by the millions.

Anglers in Canada don't regularly fish specifically for sauger and when they do catch one, most people think they have caught a small walleye. The sauger has firm, white flesh which some people prefer over the walleye. Saugers can be caught by using the same baits and presentations that catch walleye.

As is often the case in this high tech world of ours, research and education is important in every field including the art of sportfishing. We hope that the glossary at the back of the book helps to clarify some of the words and descriptions used throughout this book. With this added knowledge, we believe the angler will in turn become a more successful walleye fishermen. Read, learn and enjoy.

Chapter 1

The Fish

Description

The walleye being part of the perch family, is characterized by rough scales, a long cylindrical body, and a distinct spiny, dorsal fin. Sharp canine teeth line both the upper and lower jaw; a feature which causes the walleye to be known as a predator fish. Another thing you'll notice, walleye lack scales on the head.

The colour of the walleye varies according to it's size and habitat. Smaller walleye can have distinctive bands across their back and down their sides resembling those of a perch. However, these markings are rare in adult fish.

Most adult walleye weighing upwards of two pounds have a green to black back and yellow to gold sides. The dorsal fin is dark in colour with a characteristic black patch where the first dorsal fin meets the second dorsal fin. This dorsal fin is known for its predominant sharp spines. The second dorsal fin has 20-22 rays. The forked tail of the walleye has a milk-white patch on the lower lobe. This prominent tip is quite often the first part of the walleye, that is seen by the angler as he reels the fish in.

The pelvic and anal fin can be clear to yellow orange in colour, with a distinctive white edge on the fins. The anal fin usually has twelve to thirteen soft rays. In turbid waters the walleye will appear faded to a variety of grey shades and may still have a slight yellow colour. In clear water with rocky or weedy bottoms, the walleye will be brightly marked. It's here that the belly is usually light coloured blending into an olive colour- green or brassy - on their sides and back.

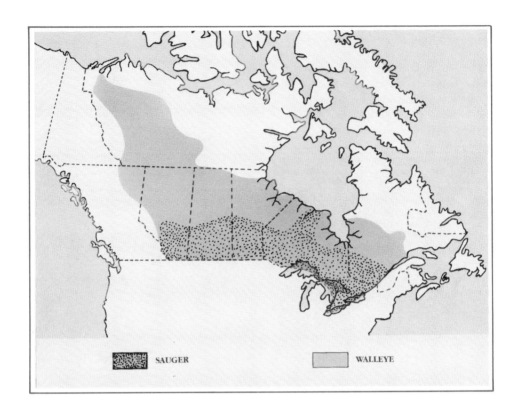

The walleye can be found from Quebec to British Columbia and as far north as the Arctic Circle in western Canada. The blue walleye can be found in some of our Great Lakes, and in northern Ontario as well as Quebec. Walleye are stocked in many waters across Canada and have been introduced in many bodies of water where natural barriers have prevented walleye populations from establishing themselves.

Habits

The walleye is basically a cool water and deep dwelling fish that can adapt to living in shallower, warmer eutrophic lakes. Spawning occurs right after the ice disappears in a lake, when the water temperatures approach 50 degrees Fahrenheit. With spring around the corner, walleye will be the first fish to move to the spawning grounds. Fast water, hard shoals and rocky shorelines make up the bulk of the spawning grounds. Most of the spawning takes place at night and it's common for one large female to spawn with as many as four to six smaller males. Walleye do not use a nest to spawn. The fish will spawn over extensive gravel or rubble areas and even over weed growth. Fluctuating water conditions can be lethal for incubating eggs in the spring of the year. After spawning, walleye require a period to recuperate before occupying their summer areas.

During the summer months walleye will move to various areas in a body of water. Some will live in the deeper parts of these lakes, while other fish still associate with the shoreline and vegetation. The walleye prefers summer temperatures of less than 80 degrees Fahrenheit. Some walleye constantly migrate and can travel as many as 20 miles in a short period of time. Other walleye remain suspended in lakes and follow schools of lake herring all season long. Generally speaking, these fish like a large lake area with a depth of more than ten feet.

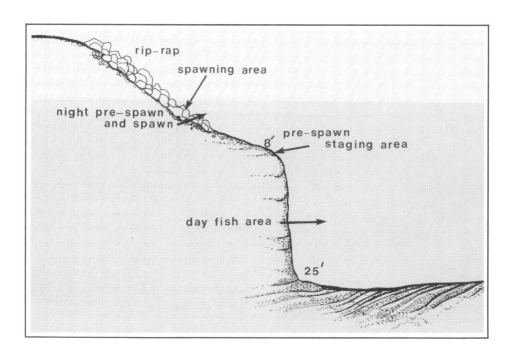

During the fall months walleye will be drawn to moving water and will start roaming the shallower shorelines in search of food. It's at this time that some of the biggest walleye are caught, since they feed quite heavily just prior to ice-up. In the winter months walleye will be found close to the fish they feed on. It's common to catch walleye in as little as three feet of water, or in 90 feet of water when fishing for lake trout in both depths.

Life History

For the walleye, life begins from a 25 to 700,000 egg hatch. Their spawning areas are usually a tributary stream, a shallow area of a river or a desirable shoal area of the lake. They do prefer clear water over five feet in depth that has a rubble or gravel area. However, for prime conditions the spawning area will likely have a current, so that the eggs can be kept clean and oxygenated.

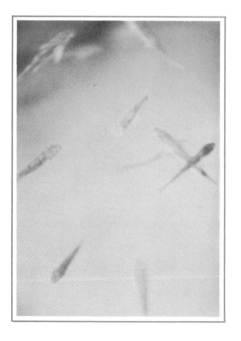

Spawning occurs right after the ice disappears, or when the water reaches the preferred temperature of 45 to 50 degrees Fahrenheit. The adult female will move into the spawning area where she will wait for the males. Most of the spawning takes place at night. The males establish trashing movements when the eggs and milt are being emitted simultaneously. Remember, walleye do not use a nest to spawn. The fish will spawn over extensive gravel or rubble areas and even over weed growth. In this process approximately 95% of the eggs will be fertilized and fall to the bottom. After spawning, no protection is given by the parents. Therefore, it is easy to understand that even with prime conditions, only five to twenty percent of the eggs will hatch in twelve to eighteen days, depending on the water temperature.

The three things that can greatly affect the hatching odds are: 1) heavy winds, 2) heavy currents, 3) dirty water. After hatching the walleye fry look very thin and are usually approximately 1/2 inch in length. The fry drift about absorbing the yolk sac to gain strength. They later feed on microscopic organisms called zooplankton. When they are several inches long they make their way to deeper water. During the summer months the walleye will move to various areas in the body of water they are in. Fish now become their primary diet and if conditions are right, at the end of the summer the walleye should be four to twelve inches long. The farther south, the longer the growing season is. Cooler waters will slow the rate of metabolism and therefore walleye will eat less in the winter months.

One out of every 10,000 walleye live to be older than one year. After the first year one out of every two walleye will live to become a mature fish. It usually takes four to five years for the average walleye to reach twelve to fifteen inches in length. A fourteen inch walleye usually weighs around one pound. Walleye over fourteen inches in length usually gain a pound for every two inches they increase in length. Therefore, a fourteen pound walleye would be approximately 36 inches long.

Characteristics

Walleye are roaming fish that can travel miles in a single day. One of the most important factors that governs their feeding activity is the amount of sunlight that is penetrating into the water. Walleye have a thin layer of tissue covering their eyes, which is extremely sensitive to light intensity. These fish will often use wood, large rocks and heavy vegetation to get away from the bright light in shallower water. Ideal environments for walleye are large, shallow lakes with turbid water. Water clarity from one to three feet is ideal. In these lakes walleye will be able to feed all day long. Walleye that inhabit lakes with very clear water may be restricted to feeding at low light intervals at dusk, at dawn and at night. In clear water lakes walleye can be found near deep water structure and weedbeds in depths from 20-40 feet. In shallow turbid lakes walleye can be caught in 2 to 3 feet of water in the middle of the day. Visibility is one of the most important factors which determines the size of a walleye "strike zone". The strike zone is the distance in which a walleye will detect and attempt to capture its prey when it decides to feed. Walleye will have the largest strike zone under low light conditions and in open water. When there is strong light intensity or no light intensity, the size of the strike zone will be smaller.

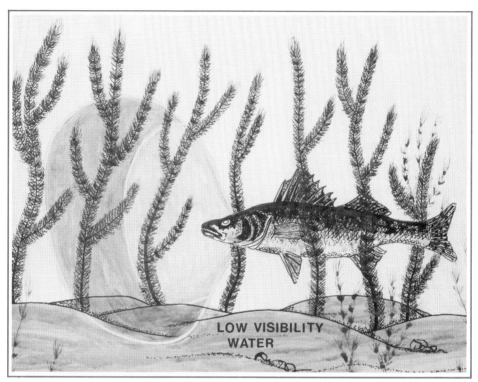

LOW VISIBILITY
WATER

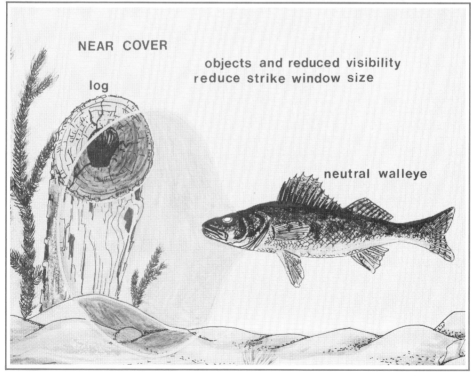

NEAR COVER

objects and reduced visibility
reduce strike window size

log

neutral walleye

Walleye are piscivorous, meaning that they feed primarily on other fish. Insects, aquatic animals, crustaceans and amphibians are also part of their diet. Immature walleye will start by feeding on invertebrates and as they start to grow larger their diet will change to small fish. At the same time, these fish change their feeding habits from being mid-depth/surface feeders to bottom feeders. In warmer lakes, yellow perch are the mainstay of the walleye's diet. Rock bass, sunfish, small bass, catfish and other readily available small fish are eaten by walleye. Walleye are not known for being voracious feeders. When angling for these fish, they usually take live bait or artificial lures very slowly, making it difficult at times for the fisherman to detect a "hit". Northern pike and muskies are the most dangerous predators for the walleye. These fish will regularly feed on walleye.

Walleye live in harmony with perch, northern pike, muskies, smallmouth bass and largemouth bass. It's common to catch all these different species from a particular lake in a specific area.

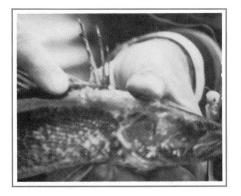

Senses

Probably the most well developed sense that the walleye possesses is the sense of vision. Walleye have a layer of skin covering their eyes called the "tapetum lucidum" which is very sensitive to light. Since walleye are extremely light sensitive as we have already discussed, in clear shallow water, during strong sunlight they will be forced to seek cover, or to venture into deeper water that will filter out the sun's harmful rays. During low light conditions and on windy days walleye can remain in shallow water. A walleye's light sensitive eyes are most functional at night. This is the reason why many walleye throughout North America do much of their feeding in low light.

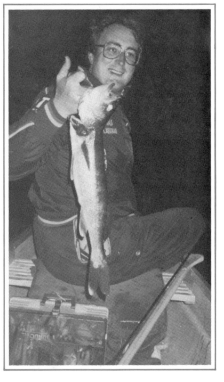

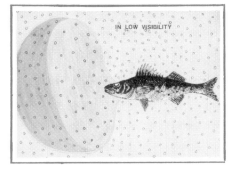

Walleye can discern colour to a degree. The most visible colours to walleye are shades of green, yellow and orange. Fluorescent colours will be much easier seen than the natural colours at any depth.

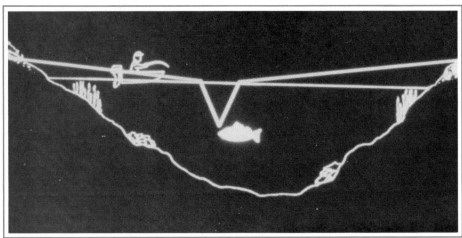

Walleye have a well developed sense of hearing and vibration. They are equipped with lateral lines and ears which can detect the slightest sounds and vibrations underwater. Walleye are able to sense the smallest erratic vibrations from a crippled baitfish to loud danger waves from alien objects such as outboard motors and banging in boats. Many times walleye will detect the vibrations from baitfish or an artificial lure previous to seeing or smelling it. It's important to note that when fishing shallow water, many walleye fishermen will anchor or drift over these fish, rather than troll which may scatter them very quickly.

Chapter 2

Habitat

Habitat

Southern Lakes (Eutrophic)

A variety of populations of walleye can be found in these lakes. They can vary from: 1. shoreline fish, 2. weedbed/ weedline fish and 3. deep water structure relating fish. We will discuss each habitat in detail.

Shoreline fish

In many southern lakes that have a water depth averaging less than 20", algae blooms and stained water is frequently found. Water clarity of three feet or less is common. Under these conditions vast numbers of walleye adapt to being in fairly shallow water including shorelines and shallow-water flats. Vegetation and/or wood may or may not be present.

Immediately after spawning many walleye will migrate to these shallow water areas to recover from their spawning activity. If the fishing season opens and the shallow water walleye are in this phase, fishing can be very difficult until these walleye begin their normal late spring and summer activity. Light intensity and the condition of the surface water are the two main factors governing the location of these fish and their activity levels. Many fishermen refer to walleye "activity moods" as being "postive, neutral or negative". When walleye are very active, swimming suspended and feed they are described as being "positive fish" or "active".

Probable

Very Probable

series of
semi-horizontal logs

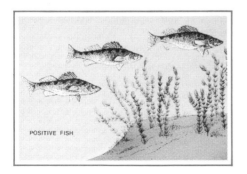

POSITIVE FISH

Neutral or Negative Fish

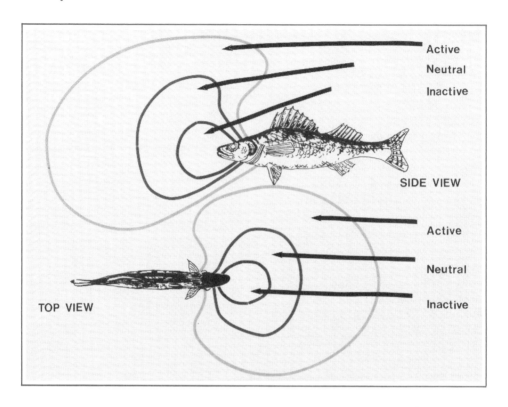

Walleye that are not active, but that will move to attack prey if it comes into range can be called "neutral fish". During strong light intensity periods, or during sudden cold fronts, walleye can become "negative fish". These fish are "in-active" and will be stationary lying on the bottom in deeper water or right in heavy vegetation. During mid-day and bright sunlight periods, these fish will either move to slightly almost inactive on the bottom, or move to areas where they can get some shade and protection from the strong light intensity. If the surface water is flat this will increase the amount of light intensity penetrating the surface, thereby, restricting the walleye movements.

On the other hand, if there are winds causing the water surface to be choppy or even rougher, this will decrease the amount of light intensity penetrating the shallow water, thus allowing the walleye to be more active. Under low light conditions such as dawn, dusk and during overcast days these walleye will be active all day long. If certain lakes experience long periods of bright sunny days the only productive times to fish may be early in the morning, late in the evening or during the night. Under bright sunlight conditions, fishing during algae blooms, or in stained water from muddy creeks or clay banks can produce steady walleye action when other areas in adjacent shallow water may be un-productive.

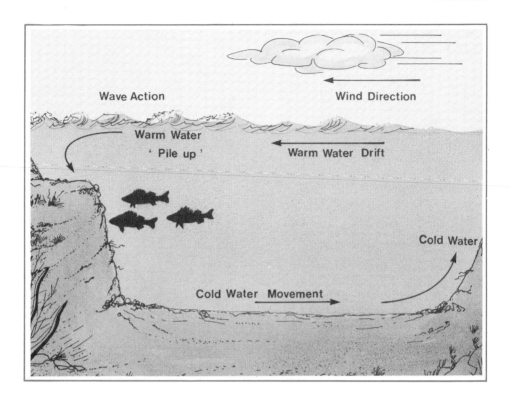

Wave Action

Wind Direction

Warm Water ' Pile up '

Warm Water Drift

Cold Water

Cold Water Movement

Walleye are regularly caught near shore or by piers. They will migrate considerably along these shorelines moving on and off shallow-water flats. At different times of the year these fish can be heard feeding on baitfish close to the surface of the water in these areas. In many lakes where golden shiners are present during certain times of the year, the shiners will swim within feet of the shallow shorelines to spawn. This usually occurs one to three weeks after the regular walleye season opens. It's at this time that these shorelines are invaded by feeding walleye converging on the spawning golden shiners. Most of this activity takes place at night and cottagers that are aware of this annual event catch their limit right off their docks. The large eyes of these fish are unique in that their glassy cast will shine under light at night.

During the fall turnover when the vegetation in these southern lakes begins to die, walleye will migrate more intensely and will venture into extremely shallow water. On many southern lakes fisherman can catch limits of walleye at night using surface lures and casting them along cattail edges or swampy shorelines. Migration along the shorelines reaches its peak in November just before most of the regular walleye fishing season closes.

29

At this time of year river mouths will attract thousands of walleye every evening. For the fisherman, most of the action is fast and furious, but quick to end with several fish being caught in a short period of time, followed by several hours of unproductive fishing waiting for more migrating fish to move up these rivers. Dams and other obstructions on river systems are areas that will hold high numbers of walleye especially at night during late fall.

As soon as southern lakes start to freeze over, walleye activity reaches its peak. The walleye that are in these shallow water areas in lakes are very easily caught. As the lakes become ice covered these walleye will move into slightly deeper water found adjacent to shorelines and shallow water flats. Their daily activity levels will vary and fish can be caught throughout the day.

Weedbed/Weedline fish

The second population of walleye will be found near the weedy areas in these shallower, southern lakes. Lakes that have a healthy population of northern pike and muskie will have less concentrated schools of walleye in these weedy areas. In these lakes northern pike will usually overtake the weedbeds and larger northerns and muskies will cruise the weed edges in search of food. In those lakes where walleye will not have to compete with northern pike, walleye can live in harmony with bass, muskie and a variety of coarse fish.

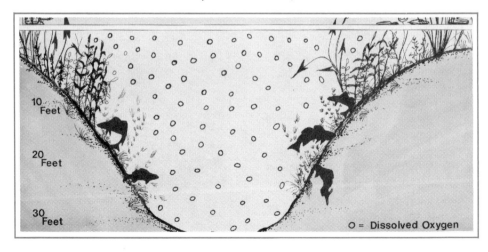

10 Feet

20 Feet

30 Feet

O = Dissolved Oxygen

As soon as the aquatic vegetation starts growing in these lakes, certain groups of walleye will move in. Early in the season these walleye will use the weed growth to shelter themselves while they go through their recovery stage.

Later on in late spring and early summer these walleye will use the vegetation as ambush cover to attack their prey and also as sunlight cover to protect their eyes from strong light intensity. During strong light intensity, the walleye will drop down near the bottom and will remain in the thick weed areas. It's at this time that they will be least active. During low light conditions the walleye will move to open pockets in these weedbeds and they will also cruise near the surface of the water, or be suspended at mid-depth in search of food. Many walleye will move to the outside edges of these weedbeds when they are actively feeding and as the day progresses they will work their way to the inside of these weed areas.

Weedbed and weedline fishing will be most productive in early summer when there is limited weed growth on a lake, thus making these walleye very concentrated. During mid-summer many of these southern lakes have vast weed areas, which can make fishing for these walleye very difficult. This group of walleye will be more localized and they will migrate within the weed areas or from weedbed to weedbed, rather than migrate along miles of barren shoreline.

During the fall as the vegetation starts to die these walleye will again become more concentrated in and along the remaining weedbed and weedline areas. During the winter on those southern lakes that have an extended ice fishing season, some of the best walleye fishing in shallow water takes place right in these remaining weedbeds, or along the weed edges.

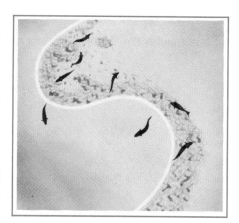

Deep-Water Structure Relating Fish.

The third main population of walleye in these southern lakes will relate almost exclusively to deeper water structure, from ten to thirty feet in depth. It is the deep water structure that will draw the early post-spawn walleye to recover in these areas first. In many lakes the deep water structure will be the most consistent producing area for steady walleye action.

Locating these deep water structures is the most difficult part in finding these deeper water walleye. These fish will be drawn to underwater structures such as a five-foot or steeper drop-off or underwater hump. Classic deep water structures are shoals, sunken islands and bars. The biggest advantage in locating deeper water walleye populations is that these fish are affected very little by varying light conditions or surface water conditions. These fish will migrate within the deep water areas usually travelling from structure to structure. During mid-summer these fish will move on and off a particular structure with regularity. During low light conditions they will be found on the bottom adjacent to this structure. Intense weather movements such as hot or cold fronts will cause these fish to be less affected and may be more easily caught then the shallower water walleye. During the fall and winter months these "holes" can attract thousands of deeper-water migrating walleye.

Northern Lakes (Mezo-Oligotrophic)

Typical northern lakes have steep, rocky shorelines characterized by deeper water. Many of these lakes may have an average depth of 40-80 feet with vegetation being limited to isolated areas in shallower water, where it is usually sparse. In these oligotrophic lakes walleye activity will be associated to; structure, bottom type, baitfish and water temperature.

Many of the post-spawn walleye will move from their spawning areas to shallow water structure between 10-15 feet in depth. Other walleye after spawning will recover in deeper water anywhere from 15-30 feet in depth. As the walleye start to become more active in late spring and early summer, they will usually follow these three basic patterns: 1. structure; 2. bottom type; 3. water temperature/bottom type.

Structure

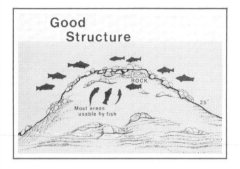

Since the water in northern lakes is usually much clearer than southern lakes, walleye activity in shallow water will be limited to low light conditions. Early in the morning, late in the day, during the night and on overcast days are the best times to fish the shallower areas. Ideal shallow water structure consists of island shorelines and rock piles close to deep water, bars and points. During bright days walleye in these lakes will move to slightly deeper structure from 15-30 feet in depth. In many mezo and oligotrophic lakes, deep water humps can attract some of the largest walleye. Humps, that are 30 feet high and are found in water that is 60 feet deep, are ideal "big fish" attractors. The most productive deep water humps will be found close to shallower water structure.

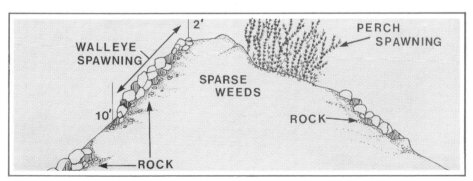

In northern lakes walleye that associate with structure will either migrate from one structure to another, or they will be home-bodies over deeper water structure.

The majority of northern walleye will be attracted to gravel, small rock structure, or large solid rocks. Timing for fishing different bottom types can be very important. Walleye in northern lakes can have predictable activity schedules. Therefore; the angler should fish different bottom types at certain times of the day to determine which group of walleye "turn on" to the different bottom type.

Bottom-Type Relating Fish

In many northern lakes, bottom type can be a main feature when trying to locate walleye. Early in the season soft bottom areas such as silt, mud, or sand may draw many walleye. It is usually in these areas that wood or vegetation will be found. Some walleye will be attracted to this feature all season long; some only during their recovery period and early summer phase.

Water Temperature/Bottom-Type Relating Fish

In most southern lakes baitfish inhabit shallower water along shorelines, vegetation or other cover. This is true in northern lakes as well, but in many cold water lakes, the only forage fish that are present may inhabit open water areas constantly moving through these bodies of water. Fresh water herring also known as ciscoe, whitefish and some of the shads can be commonly found in these northern lakes. These fish are regularly eaten by lake trout and pike and usually associated with certain water temperature zones. These baitfish are usually found cruising in large schools either above or below the thermocline (the preferred temperature zone).

Certain populations of walleye will learn to feed mainly on these colder water fish. It can be common to fish over water that is 100-200 feet deep and to catch walleye suspended 10-20 feet below the surface.

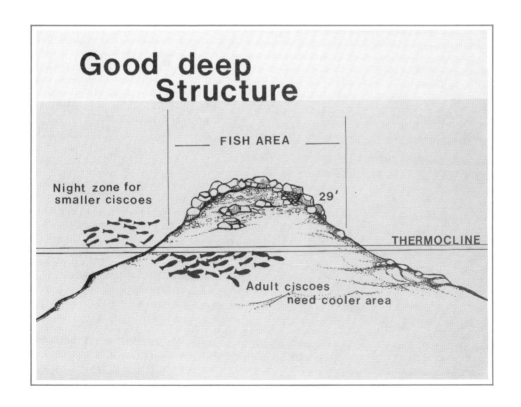

Good deep Structure

FISH AREA

Night zone for smaller ciscoes

29'

THERMOCLINE

Adult ciscoes need cooler area

To locate these deeper water schools of baitfish, a fish finder is a must. It will be the only tool to show you when you are over these baitfish schools and to show you how far down they are. These deeper water walleye may be the hardest population of walleye to catch consistently, since they can travel miles migrating after schools of baitfish.

While fishing for this particular population of walleye, winter or summer, it is common to catch lake trout, whitefish or herring in the same areas using the same baits.

Rivers

River systems can be very different to fish than lakes. Size and flow of a river is the first thing to consider. "Walleye in smaller rivers with less flow can be easily located. In the spring these fish can be found throughout these smaller rivers. Bends, flats, heads of pools and tail-ends of pools will be very productive. Early in the spring, the most productive areas in these smaller rivers will be below major obstructions such as waterfalls, rapids and dams. As the season progresses, these walleye will be found in the deeper pools during the day and in the faster, shallower water during the night.

Larger rivers can be described as moving lakes. In eastern Canada, the St. Lawrence River is a perfect example. Lake St. Francis and Lake St. Louis are just two of the lakes located on the St. Lawrence River. Both lakes have an average current of 10-15 miles per hour. In certain areas these river/ lakes can have currents of 30 miles per hour. In such large rivers, walleye can be found near aquatic vegetation, but the majority of the walleye will associate with major structure points that create underwater current breaks.

"Reefs" can be the number one attracting structure in strong currents. Walleye in these river systems will lay hugging these reefs, either on the bottom or suspended. When these fish become active, they will move in and out of the faster, shallower water areas or major weedbeds and weedlines. Being able to "read the water" can be one of the most important tools in locating fish in large rivers. Smooth water followed by ripply or choppy water usually will indicate a sudden depth change. Boils on the surface mixed with ripples can indicate large boulders and a "up and down" bottom. Navigation channels and deeper water flats in 20-30 feet will hold many walleye throughout the season. Most large river channels will have a good mixture of deep water (40-60') with flats of 20-30 feet in depth, on either side of these channels. Seasonal movements of these fish will depend almost entirely on current flows and light intensity. It is common for large river walleye to migrate up smaller rivers and streams in the spring and fall. Ice fishing takes place in isolated areas on river systems and only anglers familiar with ice thicknesses and currents should venture out during this time of the year.

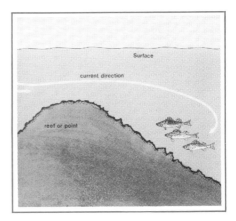

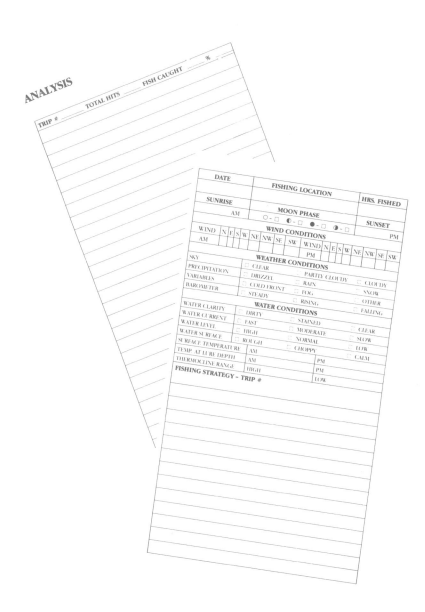

ANALYSIS

TRIP #   TOTAL HITS   FISH CAUGHT   %

DATE	FISHING LOCATION		HRS. FISHED

SUNRISE

AM

MOON PHASE

○ - □   ◑ - □   ● - □   ◐ - □

SUNSET

PM

WIND CONDITIONS

WIND	N	E	S	W	NE	NW	SE	SW	WIND	N	E	S	W	NE	NW	SE	SW
AM									PM								

WEATHER CONDITIONS

SKY			
PRECIPITATION	CLEAR	PARTLY CLOUDY	
VARIABLES	DRIZZEL	RAIN	CLOUDY
BAROMETER	COLD FRONT	FOG	SNOW
	STEADY	RISING	OTHER
			FALLING

WATER CONDITIONS

WATER CLARITY			
WATER CURRENT	DIRTY	STAINED	
WATER LEVEL	FAST	MODERATE	CLEAR
WATER SURFACE	HIGH	NORMAL	SLOW
SURFACE TEMPERATURE	ROUGH	CHOPPY	LOW
TEMP. AT LURE DEPTH	AM		CALM
THERMOCLINE RANGE	AM	PM	
	HIGH	PM	

FISHING STRATEGY – TRIP #   LOW

Chapter 3

Fishing Patterns

Fishing Patterns

Southern Lakes

Once you have decided which body of water you are going to fish, you must decide which group of walleye you are going to go after. You can choose from a number of patterns:

1. River mouths
2. Flats
3. Weedbeds/weedlines
4. Shoreline and points
5. Deep water structures

Rivermouths Pattern

In many southern lakes early in the season the number one pattern to fish is river mouths. Obstructions on rivers such as dams, waterfalls and shorelines adjacent to river and stream mouths can be very productive. These areas can be fished effectively during the day from a boat and sometimes at night from shore. Trolling the deeper areas with wobbling plugs or spinner and worm/minnow combinations can be very effective.

Drifting over the shallower areas with live-bait rigs and artificial rubber twisters as well as hair jigs will produce many walleye, especially during mid-day when their activity levels may be low. The adjacent shorelines can be worked by casting lures or still fishing with live bait. Backtrolling will work well in all these different areas slowing down the presentation while at the same time covering the most water.

Flats Pattern

A second very effective pattern is to fish flats which are usually found off the river mouths or on wind affected sides of a lake, where sediment deposits have been building up over a long period of time. Generally speaking, flats are wide areas that have a consistent depth with a distinct edge of surrounding deep water. Most flats will be anywhere from three to ten feet in depth, some may be as deep as twenty feet in depth. Flats will draw walleye throughout the day or night.

On lakes with low water clarity, flats are usually hot-spots all season long. Flats will be either barren of vegetation, or will be mottled with weedbeds. Open flats can be fished very easily by backtrolling, front trolling or drifting. Still fishing is more productive in deeper water flats. On shallow flats it is important to cover as much water as possible to find individual fish. Deeper water flats tend to hold higher concentrations of fish that at times are close together and can be easily caught still fishing.

Weedbeds and Weedlines

A third pattern is "fishing the weedbeds and weedlines". During early and mid-summer, weedbeds in southern lakes will hold a large majority of a lake's walleye population, especially if there are no pike in the lake. Weed fishing for walleye may require using special techniques such as "rip-jigging" also known as "snap-jigging". Artificial hair jigs and rubber grubs may be the only lures that will penetrate these weed areas.

'Skimming' at Night

electric motor

lure travels above weeds

The jigs are cast right into the weed bed choosing open pockets as targets. The jig is worked up and down until you hit a weed. That's when the rod is snapped in an upwards direction very quickly, so that the jig cuts right through the vegetation and is allowed to fall free to the bottom. If there are definite holes in a thick weedbed "flipping" jigs and small rubber worms into these pockets can be very effective. Most of the hits occur when the jig is on the way down and fishermen will only feel a heavier weight when they go to lift the jig up. That's the signal to set the hook. If the weedbeds are more sparse, live bait fishing can bring success. Many fishermen will use live bait threaded on a dressed, or undressed jig head and will work this combination on the bottom. Float fishing with live bait in-between weed patches is most effective when fish are less active.

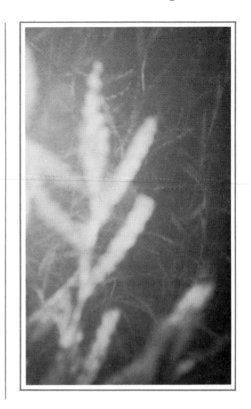

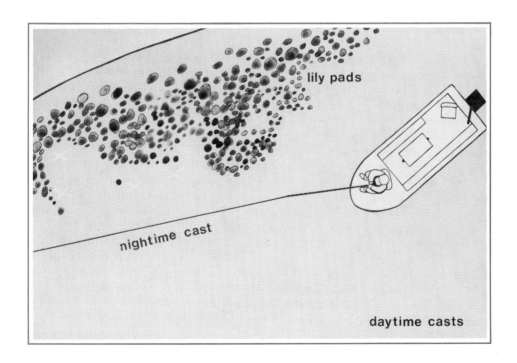

43

Standard float rigs, or sliding float rigs will work well with worms, minnows, leeches and other live bait. Weedlines are usually much easier to fish. These will be most productive early and late in the day. Shallow water weed edges are usually easy to follow with the naked eye, since the vegetation usually comes to the surface. In deeper water where you cannot visually see the weed line, a flasher or graph must be used to stay on the weed line. The most important factor when fishing weedlines is to keep your bait within a few feet of the weed edge. Many people will troll a variety of artificial lures and live bait combination just off these "weedlines". Casting lures and still fishing parallel to the weed edge also works very effectively.

Shoreline and Points Pattern

Shallow open-water fishing off of shorelines, points and weed areas can be very productive when trying to locate a cruising school of walleye. Most anglers will find water between 6 to 12 feet and they will either start drifting or trolling over these areas. Once fish are located, these passes or "runs" as they are sometimes called, can produce fish after fish. However, trolling is the most popular technique for open, shallow water fishing.

Deep Water Structures Pattern

Deep open water fishing is a popular method used by many still fishermen. Anchoring a boat near structure and either using live-bait on the bottom or using artificial jigs and grubs can be very effective. Vertical jigging is one of the most efficient ways to fish "deep holes" in southern lakes. Electronic equipment must be used to locate these deep water areas. Deep water fishing can require more patience than shallow water fishing, since many times walleye will be present, but they will only "turn on" at certain times of the day and then they will turn off again.

Northern Lakes

Most of the patterns used in fishing northern lakes will relate to deeper water. There are six basic patterns that we will be discussing:

1. Shorelines
2. Bays
3. Island/ Rock-piles
4. Points
5. Deep holes
6. Suspended fish

Shorelines

The most common pattern to locate walleye in northern waters is to either front-troll or back-troll along shorelines. This can be done by going along the mainland shoreline or by trolling along island shorelines. Most of the trolling will be done within 15 to 30 feet out from the shoreline in water that can be anywhere from 10 to 20 feet in depth. Deep diving plugs are very effective for "bouncing off the bottom" in deeper water. Hair jigs or rubber grubs topped with live bait are probably the most popular artificial/live bait combo when back-trolling. Bottom walking weights rigged with a long leader can be used to troll shallow running lures close to the bottom or to back-troll live bait rigs. Steep dropping shorelines will usually be the most productive when fishing this pattern.

Bay Pattern

Another very popular pattern when fishing northern lakes is to fish the large and small bays which are on the main lake. Drifting or trolling the inner bay shorelines is a fast and effective way of locating cruising fish. Extreme shoreline changes such as from steep rock drops to flat or beach like shorelines will indicate a change in bottom structure. These changes are usually found where the lake shoreline turns into a bay. The back ends of bays will usually have sand or silt shorelines with some vegetation. These are early morning and late evening hot-spots.

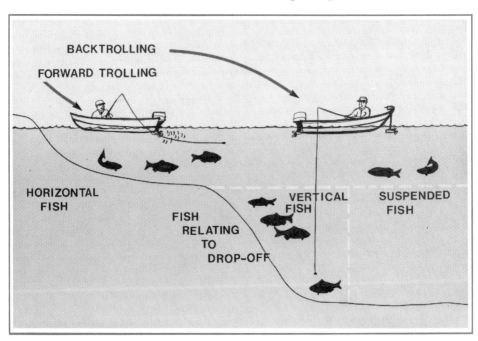

Islands/Rock Pile Pattern

Fishing structure that can be visibly seen in the open lake can be productive throughout the day. Single islands, clusters of islands and rock piles or rock outcrops which are surrounded by deep water will produce good walleye fishing all day long. When fishing these areas it is very important to test all sides of the islands or rocks. The direction of the wind, currents that are present and shade can all have an effect on where the walleye will be feeding. As a rule of thumb, early in the morning the shaded sides of islands are most productive tight to the shoreline. As the day progresses fish may start to cruise or move to slightly deeper water off these structures. A variety of techniques can be used to fish these areas. Most walleye fishermen will front or back-troll to locate these fish. Once the fish are located, casting, anchoring even still fishing can be very productive.

Point Pattern

Fishing mainland points on northern lakes can be a very productive pattern. Points that extend for longer distances into deep water are usually the most productive. Shorter points will usually hold some fish, but they may not hold as high a concentration of fish as the longer points. Points that extend adjacent to deep bays are good walleye attractors, since this may be the first major structure change that the walleye cruising out of these bays will encounter. Points that extend out into deep holes can act as "underwater highways" for walleye. Walleye will follow the underwater point right up to the shoreline. Casting, jigging, drifting and still-fishing are the most productive ways to fish these points.

Deep Holes

Some of the deepest holes in northern lakes will attract high numbers of walleye, especially in mid to late summer when water temperatures reach their highest. Fish-finders are a must when locating these "holes". Believe it or not, sudden deep water changes from 20 to 50 feet can hold thousands of walleye in different lakes. These fish will usually be neutral (semi-active- and may require extremely slow moving presentations to make them hit. Anchoring and vertical jigging or still fishing with live bait on the bottom will be the most productive methods to catch these fish.

Suspended Deep-Water Pattern

The last pattern that is not very well known by many Canadians is to fish open deep water areas for suspended walleye. These walleye will be constantly cruising and following schools of freshwater herring or other cold-water baitfish. Again a fish-finder is a must for locating these suspended fish. In many lakes fishermen can consistently catch large walleye weighing four to twelve pounds by fishing this pattern. Trolling for these fish with wobbling lures is the most common technique used. In recent years many fishermen throughout Canada have been experimenting with downriggers and planer-boarding techniques to reach these suspended fish. Even though these fish are found over deep water to depths of over 200 feet, most of these cruising walleye will be only ten to twenty feet below the surface. Night time fishing for these suspended walleye can be extremely productive.

Small Rivers

There are distinct patterns to use for fishing both small and large rivers. The major patterns when fishing small rivers are:

1. Major obstructions, dams/falls
2. Trolling
3. Drifting
4. Anchoring

Major Obstructions-Dams-Falls

Man-made obstructions such as dams, breakwalls or locks are primary areas that will hold high concentrations of walleye throughout the season.

Although these areas are especially productive early in the summer and late in the fall. Many populations of walleye will be attracted to these streams and rivers to spawn and it's right after opening day that many of these walleye remain in these areas. Shore fishing can be very productive if the shoreline permits making the right presentation. Many people fish right off the dams, either jigging artificial lures or fishing live bait in the fast water. If the shorelines and dams are not accessible by shore-fishermen, a boat has to be used. Every dam or waterfall has the same basic type of water. White water at the base of the dam or falls indicate a slightly deeper bottom. Flat water immediately after the white water indicates tail-water leading to the rivers "hardpan" (the main river bed).

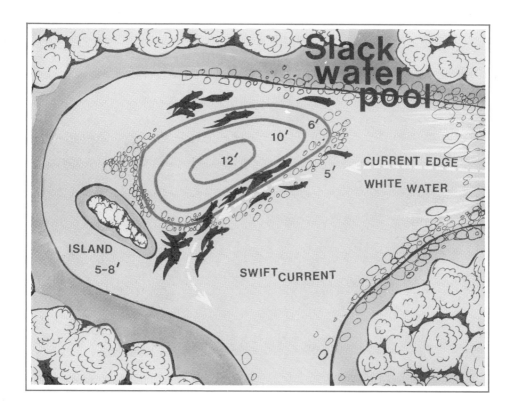

During high water periods walleye can be found scattered throughout these smaller rivers. During low water periods these walleye will be restricted to the deeper water areas. When fishing dams and waterfalls, the tail end of the main pool can be productive, as is fishing above the dam. Later in the day fishing live bait on the bottom, or jigging is productive in the white water, in the back-wash and in the main current. Daily peak fishing times at dams and waterfalls are early morning, late evening or at night.

Trolling Patterns

Trolling smaller rivers is a popular pattern early and late in the year, or during high water periods. Trolling works especially well when walleye tend to be scattered. Most anglers troll into the current so they have total control over their presentation. "River slipping" is a very popular technique which many anglers use to troll with the current. To "slip" you turn the boat around so that the engine faces the current. This technique allows you to move your bait slower than the current, thus giving you excellent control over your presentation. This method works extremely well when using live bait rigs, hair and rubber jigs on the bottom. Prime areas to troll would be straight shorelines on either side of the river as well as the inside and outside bends and flats that are created on every inside bend of the river from the deposit of silt on the bottom. Many walleyes will lie right off the front of these flats on the bottom; therefore, the most productive method for catching these fish would be trolling.

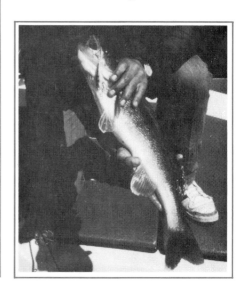

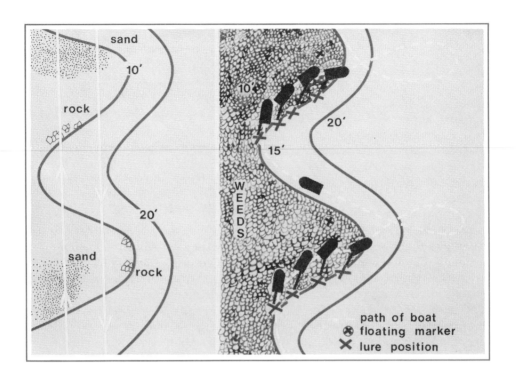

path of boat
⊗ floating marker
✕ lure position

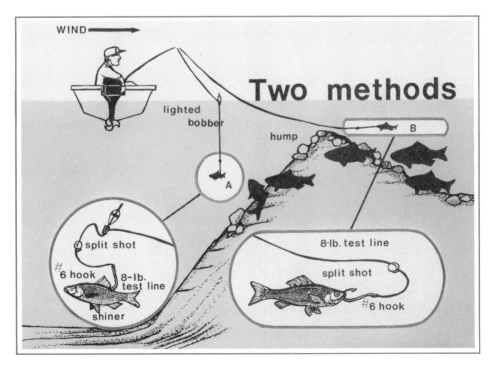

WIND ➡

Two methods

lighted bobber

hump

B

A

split shot

#6 hook   8-lb. test line

shiner

8-lb. test line

split shot

#6 hook

Drifting Pattern

Drifting a river is a very effective pattern that lets the current take you to where the fish are. A walleye fisherman must learn to read the surface of the water when he is drifting so that he can distinguish where the deeper water areas are and where large obstructions are underwater. Large boulders that create boils on the surface are hot spots to drift over. Many people make the mistake of fishing the bottom side of these obstructions and not the top. Most often walleye will be caught in front of these large boulders rather than behind because that's where the fish have first choice at food passing by. Heads of pools and tail-ends of pools can be very productive. The most important point to remember when fishing this pattern is to keep your bait right on the bottom.

Anchoring Pattern

Anchoring is probably the most efficient pattern to use when fishing deeper holes of fast water areas in a small river. Anchoring gives the walleye fisherman more time to work a certain stretch of water and it helps to make the presentation right in front of moving fish. When anchoring in a river, the boat should always be positioned down current at a 45 degree angle from the chosen fishing area. This is very important because the most effective presentation will be to cast your bait up into the current and let the moving water take the bait naturally through the stretch of water you have chosen to fish.

Under some special conditions you may want to anchor your boat up-stream from a tail end of a pool. This will enable you to let line out so that your bait can drift naturally with the current and once you see the line reaching the tail end of the pool you can pick up the slack line and be prepared to "set the hook". Drifting with live bait on a sliding sinker rig, or bouncing a jig and live bait combination on the bottom is the most effective way to cover the water while being anchored.

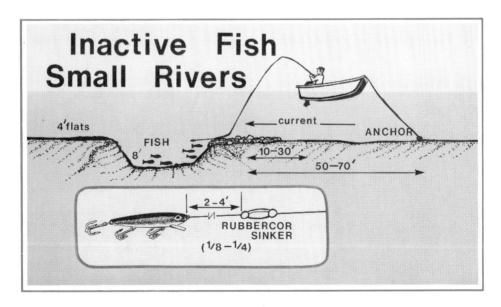

Large Rivers

Unlike small rivers, large rivers can have very strong currents and the walleye can be scattered. There are four specific patterns that can be used to successfully catch fish in these large rivers. These are:

1. Current breaks/reefs
2. Flats
3. Navigation channels
4. Weedlines

front, or just behind the reef. When they are not active, they are usually very close to the bottom. When these walleye are active they will suspend and start cruising, that's when trolling the edges is productive. When walleye around these reefs are in-active, anchoring or controlled drifting are the better methods to use. These tactics will allow your bait to stay in the strike zone as long as possible.

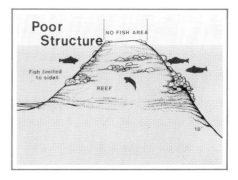

Current Breaks/Reef Pattern

Many large river systems can have water flowing anywhere from ten to thirty miles per hour. In these rivers one of the most productive patterns is to fish current breaks, such as underwater reefs. Reefs can usually be spotted by the surface water which is created when shallow water meets deeper water. Flat water followed by choppy ripples will indicate the edges of these reefs. One of the best ways to fish these reefs is to use a controlled trolling technique. It can be very important to maneuver the boat so that your lure will travel along the drop-off. The walleye that will be attracted to these breaks will lie just in

Flats Pattern

Flats ranging from depths of ten to thirty feet can be extremely productive all season long. This pattern works very well in rivers that are pike infested. Pike will compete with walleye on the major weedlines and on the current breaks, but will seldom remain on the open flats. Flats that are close to deep channels or major weedbeds or weedlines will be the most productive ones. Most of the time when walleye are located on the flat , presentation is the key factor in getting these fish to strike.

Drifting is the first choice to cover a flat when trying to locate these fish. Once the fish are located, anchoring and concentrating on a section of the flat at one time will be very productive. Many anglers will drift with bottom walking weights attached to the line, with a three-way swivel and a long leader with a rapala tied to the end. Sinkers up to two ounces in weight are used to keep the baits down. The most important points to remember when fishing any flat under moving water is to make your presentation with the current and to keep your bait on the bottom. Vertical jigging with heavy jigs and spoons can also be very effective when anchored over these fish.

Navigational Channels

Fishing the edges of navigation channels is one of the most productive patterns even under adverse weather conditions. Walleye that will cruise these deep channels will be only slightly effected by changing weather conditions. These fish will move regularly off the main channels onto adjacent structure or small flats. These channels are usually 30 to 60 feet in depth, but most of the walleye will be caught on the edges in water from 15 to 30 feet in depth. Drift fishing is the number one technique to use when fishing this pattern. Many anglers who regularly fish these large bodies of moving water will drift and jig on the bottom. "Slipping" these large areas can also be very productive. Navigation channels will produce good walleye fishing all day long and can also be very productive at night.

Coontail

Weedlines

Weedline patterns in large rivers are very productive if pike are not present in that body of water. As mentioned before, pike will compete with all other species to control weedbeds or weedlines. Pike can adjust very easily to weedlines in fast moving water. The most productive weedlines for walleye in these larger rivers will be those adjacent to large flats on the main river. Weedlines close to shore, in shallower water or on navigation channel edges will usually attract less walleye and more concentrations of pike. Weedlines in rivers are usually drifted with bottom baits.

Occasionally trolling these edges can be very productive. Downriggers can be used to fish the deeper weedlines efficiently. A weedline pattern will be most productive during early to mid-summer as well as early and late in the day.

Ice Fishing

Some of the best walleye action can be had fishing through the ice. Some of the most popular fishing patterns to use when ice fishing for walleye are:

1. Weedbeds/weedlines
2. Structure
3. Channels, flats and open water.

Even though winter fishing for walleye can be the most productive time to catch these fish, fishermen have to take heed of ice conditions and they must become familiarized with the body of water they intend to fish. The ice-fishing season for walleye usually starts the end of December in central and eastern Canada. Generally speaking, first ice and just before ice-out are the peak periods to catch lunker walleye. Ice-fishing for walleye is very easy, using simple techniques. The hardest part of successful ice-fishing is locating the fish.

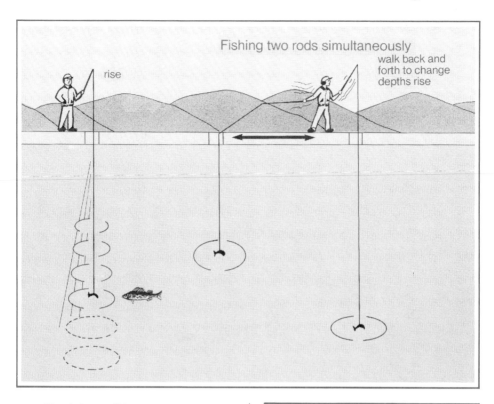

Fishing two rods simultaneously

rise

walk back and
forth to change
depths rise

Weedbeds/Weedlines

Most walleye fishermen will start by
fishing close to weed areas in a lake.
In many lakes some of the best walleye
fishing will be right in the middle of
very large weedbeds. It is common for
the serious ice-fisherman to cut many
holes trying to locate open pockets to
fish in these weedbeds.

This is where a flasher or liquid crystal
recorder can come in handy. By
placing your transducer in a plastic
bag filled with antifreeze you can get
accurate readings on both structure
and fish. This procedure will save
valuable fishing time and you'll avoid
repetitive hole drilling in favour of
some prime walleye action.

Setting up holes as "milk runs" can produce many fish from one area. This is done by cutting several holes in a given area and locating several openings in the weed bed. Once the holes are made the angler fishes each hole for a certain period of time and constantly moves from one hole to the next. Walleye will slowly move within a weedbed during a given day. They will be attracted to the open areas which will increase your chances of hooking these fish. Fishing weed edges through the ice is also part of the weedbed pattern. Weed edges are high traffic walleye paths that are used extensively during daily walleye migrations. If the ice is not very thick and the water is clear, these weedbeds and weedlines can be spotted by sight. If the ice is thick, or if it is snow covered a flasher should be used to determine open areas or weedlines otherwise the angler has to use the method of trial and error. Still-fishing with minnows on set lines or jigging with a spoon and minnow combination will be the most productive techniques to use when ice-fishing a weed pattern.

Structure Pattern

Structure patterns are very productive when ice fishing northern lakes. Most of the walleye will be found in structure from 10 to 30 feet of water. Some exceptions can be made with walleye being caught as deep as 100 feet or deeper while ice-fishing for lake trout. Structure which is in between shallower "food shelves" and deep water areas will be most productive. When fishing this pattern jigging with flashy spoons will usually be more productive than set-lines rigged with live minnows. Set-lines can be productive and two minnows should be used on each line with a "walleye rig". These structures will draw cruising fish, therefore it is very important for the fisherman to stay on the structure he is fishing and not move around too much. Most of the fishing will be erratic, with random fish being caught all day long.

Channels, Flats & Open Water

Channels and open water flats are the last popular pattern for the ice-fishing season that we will discuss. On many lakes where pike will "take-over" weed areas, walleye can be found concentrated in open water. These fish are usually active migrators covering great distances of water in a matter of days. Large schools of walleye sometimes numbering in the thousands will cruise the open water areas all winter long. Locating these fish can mean limit catches in a matter of hours. Most fishermen that find these large schools are familiar with the lake they are fishing and they will follow these migrating walleye from one end of the lake to the other.

Migrations are predictable and walleye will be found in the same general areas each winter at the same time. Jigging to cover the most water is the number one method used to find these fish. Many times by watching in the distance the ice fisherman can see other fishermen starting to catch fish, indicating that a school of fish is moving his way. This pattern reaches its peak in late winter when the schools of walleye migrate near their spawning sites. Some of the largest female walleye are caught while ice fishing at this time. The only problem with late winter fishing is that the fisherman has to be aware of ice conditions and that he must know when to keep off the ice prior to "break-up". Many fishermen angling during late winter will take canoes or aluminum boats with them onto the ice as a safety precaution.

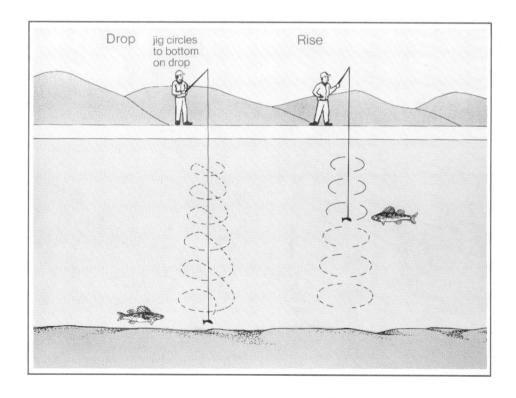

Warm Water Outflows

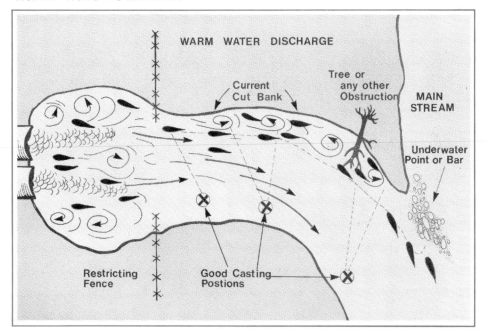

In many parts of Canada, water is used to "cool off" a variety of industrial machinery. Through this process, this water warms up before it is released back into a lake system. During the winter months when most of Canada's waters are either very cold or frozen, warm water outflows can provide some "hot" winter open-water fishing for walleye. Most of these discharges appear as large rivers with a good current. The warm water can be easily seen because it gives off steam as it mixes with the colder lake water and cold air. Walleye will usually follow baitfish which are attracted to this warmer water. These fish will also associate with current breaks and underwater structure such as bends, sand bars and rock piles. Most summer fishing techniques will work to catch walleye and once again the early morning and late evening hours are prime time fishing hours.

Chapter 4

Fishing Equipment

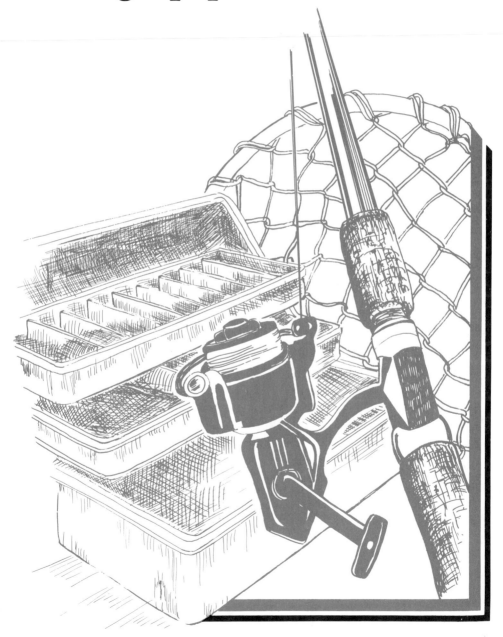

Fishing Equipment

Rods

Walleye can be caught on almost any rod which is available in North America. However, for the sportsman who considers himself more than a casual walleye fisherman, certain rods can help to increase his catch under different conditions while using various patterns and techniques.

The material of composition, rod flex, rod sensitivity, blank construction, length and weight of rods are all very important factors when trying to make a particular lure or bait presentation under diverse conditions. A rod that is designed to be used with light line for casting and drifting small lures, will not be a good rod to use for trolling or in conjunction with heavy lines and lures. On the other hand, a rod which is short, stiff and that is designed especially for jigging will not be a good rod to use with four pound test line. The rod will be overpowering the line and in many cases will break light line.

During a day's outing, the serious walleye fisherman might be fishing as many as three to five different fishing patterns to catch his fish. It is common to use both spinning and baitcasting equipment in one day's fishing. This means that the walleye fisherman should consider having three to six rod and reel outfits, each rigged with different lures, or live bait. These outfits would range from ultra-light spinning to heavy-action baitcasting gear.

Spinning Gear

With the availability of today's "hi-tech" rod materials and components, the highest quality rods on the market are in our opinion Graphite blank construction, together with hard Silicate Carbon or Graphite guides. Most of these rods are very light, but extremely strong.

We will begin by discussing "light-line" spinning rods for use with light-weight lures between 1/16 and 1/4 oz. Most walleye fishermen would classify this light a rod as an "ultra-light". They are designed to be used with two to six pound test line in open water while casting, or still fishing. Under some conditions small jigs and light line presentation will be the deciding factors for producing limit catches of walleye. Ultra-light rods can be anywhere from four and a half feet in length, to specialized twelve foot rods. When using light line, it is very important to use a rod that is flexible enough to "give" when

a fish wants to exert force. The most popular ultra-light rods are four and one half to five feet in length. The longer rods will work well with light line, but it is much more difficult to detect strikes because of the shock absorbing properties of these blanks. Berkley manufactures a series of high quality 100% graphite rods that are designed for light line use. These include the Lightning rods, Bionix rods and Series One rods.

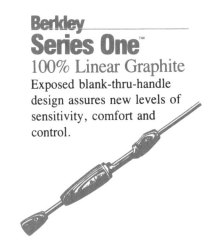

Berkley

Series One™

100% Linear Graphite
Exposed blank-thru-handle design assures new levels of sensitivity, comfort and control.

Light action spinning rods are designed to be used with lures weighing 1/8 to 1/2 ounce in weight. These rods are the mid-point between the ultra-light and medium action rods. They are also ideal when fishing open water patterns either casting or still fishing. Lengths vary, but, as a rule most light action rods are six to seven feet in length. Overall, light action rods are ideal to use for 6 to 8 pound test line.

Medium action spinning rods are the most popular all-round walleye rods. The reason they are so popular is that you can use a wide range of lure weights and line sizes. These rods are also ideal for both casting or trolling. Medium action rods are usually 5 1/2 feet to 7 feet in length. They are designed to be used with line between 6 and 12 pound test. Medium action rods can be used for jigging or fishing near weeds, but they are not designed for that special purpose.

your presentation. These rods are very stiff which makes them ideal for jig fishermen to use them for "snap or rip-jigging" in heavy weeds. They can also be used for trolling, but they are rather short and can be awkward to handle if one or more people are fishing from the same boat. These rods are usually 5 1/2 foot in length and they are frequently one piece for maximum strength and sensitivity.

Heavy action, short, stiff rods are ideal "jigging" rods for walleye. These rods are short so that the fisherman has more line control and less distance to the end of his rod tip. Short, stiff rods produce less air resistance when fishing in windy conditions. This means you can jig in rough water and still have maximum sensitivity with

Heavy action, long spinning rods in lengths from 6 to 8 feet are ideal for the dedicated walleye "trolling fisherman". These rods should be stiff enough to handle lures from 1/4 to 1/2 ounce and should be designed to handle larger capacity spinning reels, that will hold several hundred yards of line from 10 to 30 pound test. Generally speaking, these rods will have longer butts which makes them ideal to hold while trolling, but somewhat-awkward and bulky for casting.

Specialized or custom-made spinning rods are used at times by walleye fishermen under extreme conditions. Very long ultra-light rods such as "noodle rods" can be used when trying to land large walleye on very light line. When using 2 to 4 pound test line, the longer the rod, the more "torque" it will be able to exert on the fish.

When downrigging for walleye, a "composite" rod should be used. The mixture of graphite and fiberglass in the blank will give the rod elasticity, so that it can be bent considerably while being "set" on the downrigger for long periods of time. Conventional graphite rods which are not designed for downrigging should not be used because they are not designed to withstand the constant pressure of being "set" on the downrigger.

Baitcasting Rods

Baitcasting rods are generally "tougher" rods that are ideal for use in heavy weed growth, for vertical jigging and for trolling. Bait casters are ideal when casting large lures such as J-13 Rapalas, large spoons, and deep diving plugs on heavier lines. Most baitcasting rods vary from 5 to 7 1/2 feet in length. They come in a variety of actions and can be purchased as one piece, two piece or semi-collapsible as in the form of "flipping" rods.

Light action baitcasting rods should be used in open water for casting, drifting, trolling and especially for backtrolling. Recommended line weights are 6 to 8 pound test line. These rods can feel as if they are a part of your arm and will detect instantly the slightest weight, snap or tug. Most lures used with these rods should weigh from 1/8 to 1/2 ounce. These rods are usually 6 to 6 1/2 feet in length and work well with line from 6 to 10 pound test.

Berkley Grayfite

50%
GRAPHITE
COMPOSITE

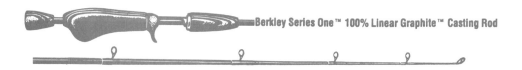

Berkley Series One™ 100% Linear Graphite™ Casting Rod

Medium action baitcasters are "multi-purpose". These rods are excellent for trolling, casting and snap-jigging. They will work well with medium action baitcasting reels that have high light line capacities. Lure weights for these rods are 1/4 to 3/4 ounces and line ranges from 8 to 12 pound test.

vertically into the water as deep as you can go without getting your hands wet. This will make a deep diving lure run up to 6 to 10 feet deeper. These rods along with 7 1/2 foot "flipping" rods will work well as trolling rods. These rods are equipped with "triggers" which aid the fisherman in holding onto the rod and also helps to give him a stronger hook set.

Longer baitcasters can be ideal for certain situations. Berkley's 7 foot "popping" or "deep cranking" rod is a good example of a specialized baitcaster. This type of heavy action, long baitcasting rod was developed to be used with ten to twenty pound test line specifically for casting deep diving plugs. With these 7 foot rods you can increase the depth a certain lure is running at, by placing your rod

Berkley Bionix®

100% High Energy Graphite

Spin-Casting Rods

These rods are available in a variety of lengths and weights and are two piece construction. They work well for beginners or people who don't want to worry about reel line tangles. The specifications for these rods are very similar to the baitcasting rods. These rods are also ideal for walleye fishing.

Fly Rods

For the fly rod enthusiast 7 to 9 foot rods with line weights ranging from 7 to 10 weight are ideal.

Ice-Fishing Rods

Most walleye ice-fishermen will either use manufactured "ice-fishing" rods such as the Normark series rods, or they will custom build their rods. All Normark ice-fishing rods have standard, single action reels which are very basic. Some of these rods have "thrumming" devices which enables the ice-fisherman to "shake" his lure by the touch of a lever. Fishermen that like using baitcasting or spinning reels will usually build very short, stiff rods ranging from 2 to 4 feet in length. Both of these systems will work well for the ice-fisherman.

Reels

Spinning

High quality reels will have smooth drag systems, high gear ratios and they will be very light for their size. Spinning reels are available in standard sizes to be compatible with rod lengths and weights.

Ultra-light spinning reels are small in appearance and are usually lightweight. These reels should have very smooth drags since they will be handling line from two to six pounds in strength. Gear ratios should be anywhere from 4:1 to 6:1 (gear ratio is the term describing the number of rotations the bail of the reel makes with each turn of the handle. For example, a 5:1 gear ratio indicates that for every turn of the handle the bail rotates five times). Some ultra-light reels are equipped with rear drag systems and trigger casting mechanisms.

Medium action reels are the most popular and they are designed to be used with six to twelve pound test line. These reels are compatible to medium action spinning rods. Smooth drag systems are not as important on these reels as they are on the ultra-light models, but they should be at least semi-smooth.

Heavy action spinning reels are designed to hold greater capacities of both light and heavy lines. These reels are ideal on trolling or downrigger rods.

Casting Reels

VM 3G

There are two baitcasting reels that are primarily used by the walleye fisherman the light action and medium action reel. Most walleye fishermen will need baitcasting reels that will be balanced on a five and one half foot to six and one half foot long rod. Some of the highest quality baitcasters are constructed from graphite. They are magnetic and come in a variety of gear ratios. Magnetic baitcasters are an asset when walleye fishing in windy conditions. To a baitcasting fisherman, strong winds, light line and light lures spell "bird nests". The magnets on these reels will slow down the spool while it is "free spooling" in a cast. Walleye fishermen that plan to do a lot of trolling should consider larger baitcasting reels with higher line capacities. These reels should have lower gear ratios for more "brute torque". Fishermen that do more casting and retrieving should consider smaller, lighter, high gear ratio baitcasting reels. Whichever reel is used on a baitcasting rod, the most important point is that the rod and reel should feel light and balanced in the angler's hand.

Fly Reels

Reels with medium line capacities such as seven to nine weight fly line are ideal. These reels should feel balanced when matched to the fly rods.

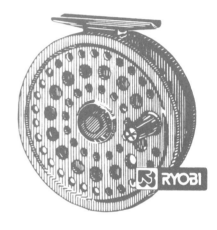

Spin-Casting Reels

Spin-casting, push-button reels are designed to be used with spin-casting rods. These reels are designed to take a variety of line weights. They are virtually trouble free because the line is contained inside the reel. This makes line tangles very rare. These are good reels for casual walleye fishermen.

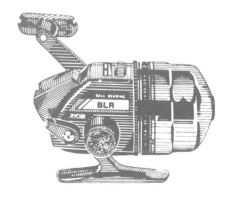

Fishing Lines

Line diameter, weight and colour can be very important to the walleye fisherman. Most walleye fishermen will use line weight ranging from six to ten pound test. When drifting on bottom it is very important to use a line that has good abrasion qualities. Berkley's Trilene XT is a good line to use when bottom fishing. This line has a hard "outer skin" which protects the outside of the line when rubbing against wood, rocks, fish teeth and fish gill rakers.

When fishing clear water the lightest and most invisible line should be used. Trilene XT green is invisible underwater and performs well.

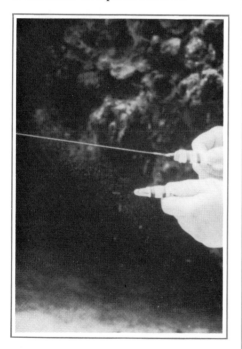

Walleye fishermen that fish at night should use fluorescent lines along with a "black light". Fluorescent line which is outside of the water will glow making line watching at night easy.

Anglers that consistently fish for deep water walleye, or that do a lot of trolling should consider using a strong low stretch line. Berkley's TriMax is an advanced TriPolymer fishing line that offers exceptional strength without sacrificing characteristics such as sensitivity, castability and fish fighting power.

Terminal Tackle

"Terminal tackle" is the general term that describes all the small attachments walleye fishermen can use to join their lure or hook to the line. The most common examples are snap swivels and leaders.

Many walleye fishermen may not realize this, but there is a great difference between run-of-the-mill terminal tackle and high quality terminal tackle. Quite a few walleye fishermen have had the experience of hooking a trophy walleye only, to loose it and find out later that their snap or snap swivel opened up on them during the fight.

When wire leaders are a must, especially in clear water, choose black wire leaders over silver wire leaders. Black absorbs light and is almost invisible underwater. Silver reflects light and is very visible underwater.

Terminal tackle should be used only if you have to. If you are drifting with live bait you normally do not require a snap or snap-swivel. If the waters you are fishing harbour northern pike or muskie you may want to use a steel leader at all times.

Berkley's lock-snaps and lock-snap swivels are one of the highest quality snaps on the market. A unique "wire over wire" lock makes Cross-Lok extra strong.

When using a jig, the jig has a tendency to "roll over" and twist the line in a certain direction. It is very important that you use some sort of swivel on the line to minimize line twists. A tip we can suggest is that you place an "in-line" swivel ten to fourteen inches up the line from your bait or lure. The swivel will reduce line twist and at the same time your jig will appear natural because there is no snap-swivel attached to it.

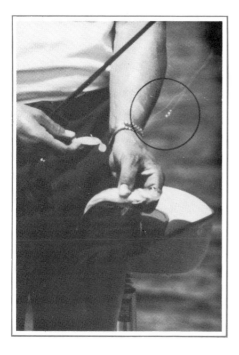

In some cases live bait fishermen will utilize a terminal tackle system known as a "walleye rig". These rigs are made up of a piece of monofilament line approximately fourteen inches long rigged with two hooks which extend away from the main line. This rig is designed to be used with a weight on the bottom to keep the two hooks suspended. This rig works especially well when fished in deep or fast water, with live bait.

Miscellaneous Equipment

Floating Markers

You can use almost any type of floating device as a marker on the surface of the water. Fishermen commonly use wood blocks, plastic bottles or blocks of foam. These can all work, but, there are floating markers that are manufactured specifically for the fisherman. Blue Fox has a light-weight marker that takes up very little storage space and is extremely visible from a distance. It is available in two sizes and comes "ready to use".

Hook Sharpener

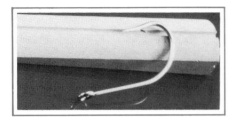

Many fishermen don't realize the importance of sharp hooks. When dealing with a basically slow hitter such as the walleye, sharp hooks are most important. Most anglers use a hook file or a sharpening stone to put a point on their hook. Berkley has an electric hook sharpener that is powered by two "C" size batteries. It's compact and will put a sharp point on even the dullest hooks. To sharpen a hook properly the angler should grind three flat sides which will form the point. Those flat sides will form three cutting edges similar to a "broad-head" on a hunting arrow which will make for better hook penetration.

Line Stripper and Hook Sharpener

Strips any reel in seconds
Built in hook sharpener

Coolers

If you plan to save walleye for eating it can be difficult to keeping these fish alive on a stringer, especially in warm water lakes. In most cases it is important to immediately "gut" the fish that will be kept for eating and place it in a large cooler filled with ice. This will ensure your catch will stay fresh until you reach the kitchen table. A cooler is also important for keeping worms, leeches and other live baits fresh during warm weather.

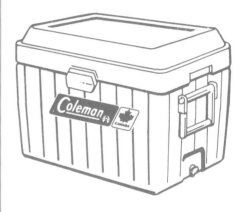

Anchors

Walleye fishermen that want to drift or still-fish in adverse weather should invest money in a good anchor or sea anchor. Lead anchors weighing between ten and twenty-five pounds are ideal for holding a position. To slow down a drift in windy weather, the fisherman can use a heavy anchor and tie the lead short so that the anchor "bounces" along the bottom. Sea anchors are devices that work like a "parachute" in the water. They trap water in a bag to slow a craft down. These items are ideal for boat control in windy weather.

Planer Boards

These mechanisms are usually made of plastic or wood and are used to deliver the anglers line away from the boat. This technique works especially well in waters where fish seem to shy away from the engine noise. At times a school of walleye will scatter to either side of the boat when a power boat approaches, especially if they are cruising close to the surface of the water. This is the best time to troll with planer boards. Planer boards are attached to a heavier "main line", usually dacron and are allowed to "swim" away from the boat. Special "release clips" connect the fishermans line to the planer board line. These clips run down the line out to the planer board, thus making it possible for the angler to troll his lure out to one side of the boat or the other. As soon as a fish strikes, the lure releases and the fisherman fights the fish out without the planer board interfering.

Many fishermen will use "Yellow

Birds" to get their line out to the sides of their boat. These "birds" are trade names for smaller and more compact mechanisms than a planer board and are attached directly to the fisherman's line. There is no release mechanism which detaches the line from the bird". When a fish hits, the "bird" disengages and just planes on the surface allowing the fisherman to fight the fish to the boat. In many southern lakes that have a lot of boat activity, planer boards are one of the best techniques to use to catch walleye consistently.

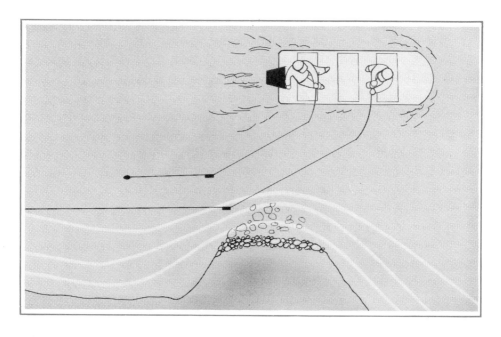

Chapter 5

Electronic Equipment

Electronic Equipment

There is a variety of electronic equipment that is available to aid the walleye fisherman. These include flashers, graph recorders, liquid crystal recorders, Loran-C guidance systems, PH meters, Colour selectors as well as trolling and temperature probes.

Fish Finders

The most important piece of electronic equipment to the walleye fisherman is the flasher or graph recorder. If a walleye fisherman does not have the use of one of these electronic aids, finding walleye is mostly guess work.

The most important function of a flasher or graph isn't to mark fish, more specifically it's to show the angler bottom depth changes, structure and vegetation, so that the fisherman can see and understand what the walleye will be relating to. A high quality flasher or graph will allow you to see depth changes even while travelling at high speeds and will aid you in maintaining a precise depth once you have located structure, fish, or weeds in a certain area. Lowrance electronics makes the highest quality flasher sonar, digital sonar units, liquid crystal graphs and computer graph recorders available to the fisherman.

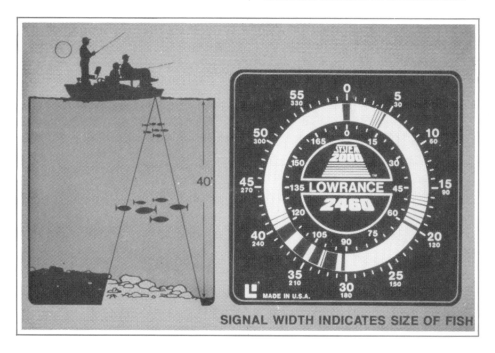

SIGNAL WIDTH INDICATES SIZE OF FISH

All in all, there are many makes of fish-finders available on the market today. In the world of fishing electronics, we have outlined a list of features that are important to have on these units. If you are in the market to up date your fish-finder or you are a first time buyer, keep these points in mind.

1. Look for units that have a high power out-put. The relationship between power and sonar performance is similar to the weak reception on your car radio. Turning up the volume won't help since you're not increasing the power of the station's signal which remains constant. In simple terms, in sonar, the more power makes for better performance.

a) Flasher sonars should have power out-puts of 150 watts P-P to 300 watts P-P. (P-P-Peak to Peak)

b) Liquid crystal graphs should have power out-puts of 300 watts P-P.

c) Computer graph recorders should have power out-puts of 1,600 watts P-P.

2. Choose flasher screens that will give you a strong signal even when the unit is exposed to strong direct sunlight. Make sure your unit has a focused-lens light-trap dial for glare-free daytime reading.

3. Look for flashers that have the appropriate scale settings for the type of walleye fishing you will be doing. For example, if you will be fishing in shallower lakes, choose scales from 0 to 30 feet or 0 to 60 feet maximum. These scales will show you the most detail in shallower waters. If you fish deeper water then you should go to a larger scale. Hi resolution as in the Lowrance units will separate targets like walleye and baitfish as close as 4 inches.

4. If price is a major factor, compare liquid crystal graphs (LCG-to computer graph recorders. The LCG units are definitely a tremendous breakthrough in sonar technology. Take pixel count for instance. Pixels are the tiny squares on the screen that light up to indicate what you're seeing underwater. Horizontal count doesn't mean much, what you have to pay particular attention to is the vertical count. When you have a versatile zoom function, you have a greater control over the resolution and what you really want to see.

You will not need to buy paper for the liquid crystal unit, but you will be forfeiting the higher resolution and permanent information of a paper graph recorder.

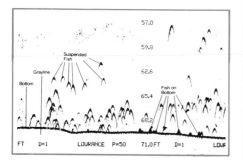

5. If you will be doing a lot of downrigger and structure fishing, you should consider a high resolution paper graph recorder. The key comparison comes with the transducers. A high operating frequency of 192 kHz with a narrow (8 degree) or medium (20 degree) beam width transducers, generally provide better definition but at shallower ranges. A lower operating frequency of 50 kHz using a 45 degree transducer will provide greater depth penetration and covers wider areas under water. This will allow you to "track" your cannon balls and rigging on the paper, so that you can relate you lure depth to possible fish markings.

6. Make sure that the recorder you are considering to buy has a "gray-line" feature. This feature will help identify the bottom contour like sand, gravel, mud, silt etc. This feature is most important when trying to locate walleye close to the bottom.

7. If you plan to use your unit at high speed, make sure it has a "suppression" setting. This will enable you to see the information clearly at high speeds with minimal interference. Make sure that your suppression system operates without reducing the sensitivity of the unit.

Artist's rendering of a typical underwater landscape. Area shown is from 25' to 35'.

X-5

Depth Range: 25 to 35 feet (zoom feature).

Each dot* represents ⅝ inches in height (· =1 dot).

Screen shown actual size.

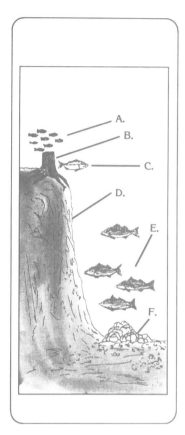

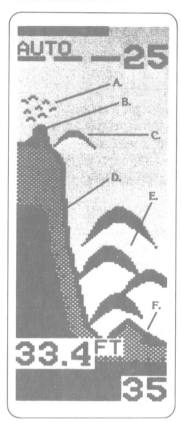

A. School of minnows	A. School of minnows
B. Stump	B. Stump
C. Fish	C. Fish
D. Bottom drop off	D. Bottom drop off
E. School of fish	E. School of fish
F. Rocks	F. Rocks

8. Look for "zoom" features on the sonars. This will enable you to take a close look at what you have recorded making your signal to appear larger on the display. Lowrance has an Eagle line of electronics which are famous for these particular zoom features.

Without a doubt, electronic "fish-finders" can improve your walleye fishing. However, knowing how to operate them properly is as important as owning one. The best way to become familiar with a fish-finder is to use it regularly. Much of the information that is displayed has to be interpreted and you develop this skill from practice.

Loran-C Guidance System

This is an electronic device which allows you to navigate using coordinates to reach a specific location. Walleye at different times of the year will hold in specific areas. Therefore, when you find a "hot spot" in a particular part of a lake, you can record it's location in the memory of these units. When you wish to return to the precise spot, you re-call the positions and the Loran-C will guide you to the exact spot, constantly giving you the distance remaining to get to that point.

MODEL 797

PH-Meter

The PH in water can vary from acidic to alkaline. Many items such as : bottom type, the presence of decomposing material, cattails, leeching of chemicals or surface run-off from the land surrounding a lake and a variety of underwater plants can affect the PH in water. PH is an important factor to consider when trying to locate walleye areas. Walleye like other game fish are very sensitive to PH changes in a body of water. To detect these variations in PH, a meter has to be used.

Factors That Affect PH?

Of course, the measurement of pH does not exist in a vacuum. Environmental conditions throughout the year affect the pH of water and cause it to change. Some of these conditions include:

Photosynthesis, the growing process of all forms of vegetation like plants and algae, raises pH. This occurs most often in sunlight, but can occur to a lesser extent in moonlight.

Rainfall lowers pH. Clean, unpolluted rainfall has a pH of about 5.6, but the acid rain (causing major problems in parts of the world) may have a pH as low as 1.7.

Pollutants in the water, depending upon their chemical make-up, have a wide range of pH readings.

Surface runoff will vary in pH, depending upon the uses of the watershed involved.

Trees and brush in the water may raise or lower pH, depending upon their type.

Decomposing organic matter, such as freshly inundated vegetation, generally lowers pH by releasing a weak acid.

Freshwater springs generally maintain about the same pH year-around, but different springs may have different pH readings.

In addition the pH of a given body of water, especially lakes, will vary with the seasons. The pH generally becomes lower in winter than at other times of the year. In spring, as the water warms and photosynthesis begins, the pH increases on the surface. As the season continues into summer, the surface pH rises and mixes downward steadily. In fall, this process reverses and the pH continues to drop back to its winter level.

Colour C-Lector

By understanding the sense of vision that the walleye possesses, the fisherman realizes that certain colours are more visible to these fish at certain depths. A colour meter tells the fisherman which colour is most visible in different water conditions. Stained, muddy, tea and clear coloured water are common in different lakes and rivers. Only certain colours will be most visible in these different water conditions with changing light intensities. Your lure size, speed and overall presentation might be right on, yet a simple colour change may be the missing link between catching walleye or not. The only way you can determine which colour will be most visible is by trial and error, or by using a colour meter.

Combo-C-Lectors have been designed to give the angler more than just lure colour. The unit also measures PH, probe depth, speed and temperature all in one unit.

Multi-C-Lector

Multi-C-Lector

The Multi-C-Lector is a console mounted unit incorporating a computer and LED light and LCD digital displays to interpret and display fishing information. The information is automatically gathered by the console controlled, transom-mounted electronic reel with a 50-foot to 150 cable and probe.

So, you know at a glance:

1. Probe Depth – This unit displays the exact depth of the probe.

2. Lure Color – This unit shows which lure color fish will prefer at any depth.

3. pH – The Multi-C-Lector tells you the pH at any depth – as well as automatically identifying and displaying the depth of a primary and secondary pH cline (breakline). It will also sound an audible signal if the probe runs through a pH sheer.

4. Temperature – This console unit will show you the temperature at the probe depth – plus it will show you the depth of a primary and secondary thermocline. It will also sound an audible signal if the probe runs through a thermal sheer.

5. Water Clarity – This unit automatically displays clarity for you. It will also show you the depth of a primary and secondary clarity cline, and sound an audible alert if you are trolling and run into a clarity sheer.

6. Probe Speed – The Multi-C-Lector interprets and displays exactly how fast the probe is moving at its depth – which may be different from boat speed due to subsurface current or boat direction changes.

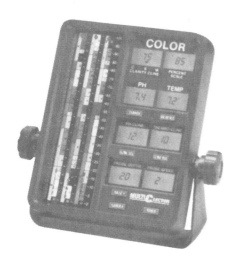

Trolling Gauges

Under certain conditions walleye will be caught with a particular bait or lure running at a certain speed. When there are changing weather and surface water conditions, it can become very difficult to troll constantly at a particular speed. A trolling gauge will show you the speed you are travelling at, so that you can adjust the throttle accordingly. Some fish finders may have this feature built into the unit.

You can easily make your own lure speed/trolling guide. Tie a line to a 2 to 5 oz. sinker to the side or stern of your boat. Note the angle at which your line is at when you get a strike on your rod. Whether you troll into the waves or with them, into the wind or not, you should be able to maintain a fairly close lure speed.

Temperature Gauge

This instrument may be very important to walleye fishermen in northern lakes. When a paper graph is not available, the next best fishing aid for walleye fisherman would be a temperature probe. You might be surprised at how easy it will be to find a temperature break like the "thermocline" and in turn find suspended walleye. There are electronic temperature probes that read from the surface temperature to 200 feet in depth. They are simple to read and are usually powered by batteries.

Chapter 6

Artificial Lures

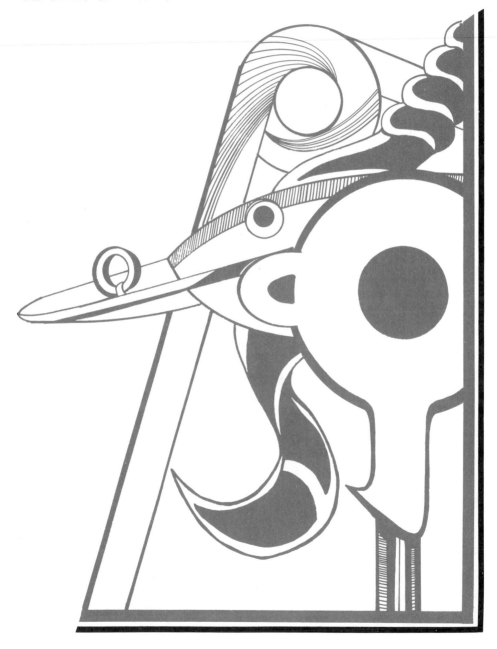

Artifical Lures

The devoted walleye fisherman must be able to efficiently use a variety of techniques which include artificial lures and live bait. Most of the walleye caught in Canada are caught using live bait. Yet, there are times when artificial lures will produce more and bigger fish than live bait.

We will discuss artificial lures under five distinct categories; wobbling lures (plugs/crankbaits), jigs, jigging spoons, spinners and flies.

Wobbling Lure Tactics:

Plugs

Most plugs are either constructed of balsa wood or polyester resin. Some specialized plugs are made out of metal. Mastering the various techniques used with different plugs can take time, but most of these lures can be just cast and retrieved to produce fish. The easiest way to fish a plug is to use a trolling technique. Most walleye plugs are between three to six inches in length, but under certain conditions larger plugs up to fourteen inches in length will produce trophy size walleye. The action of these plugs is usually a "side to side wobble". Some have a very tight-fast wobble, others have long wide wobbling action. No matter what size, these types of lures vibrate when retrieved. The most widely used plugs for walleye are those that more closely imitate the baitfish the walleye are feeding on.

Over the years the "Rapala" has established itself as "the" walleye plug. The most popular version of this lure is the one piece, short lipped model. "Count-down" models are available in the Rapala series and even though they have short lips they will sink and work at deeper depths. Other wobbling plugs that work very well are; Rapala's jointed models, Beno, Luhr Jensen Gad-A-Bout Wobbler, Bomber baits, Flatfish lures, Canadian Wiggler, Bagley baits, Thin-Fin lures, L&S Mirror Lure, Pikie Minnows (jointed and one piece), Heddons Vamp Spooks, Lazy Ike, Swim Whiz, Believer lures and Spoon-plugs.

Plug Presentation

As mentioned before these lures are ideal trolling lures, especially in shallower water or over heavy weed growth. These shallow running lures seem to have an uncanny ability to consistently catch fish. Many fishermen who troll deeper water in the ten to twenty foot range will still use these shallow running plugs, but will weigh them down by placing a 1/4 to 3/4 oz. weight about twelve to fifteen inches ahead of the lure. Gapen's Baitwalker rig is ideal to use to get these plugs to run along the bottom in deeper water.

In "fast-water" fishermen will cast these plugs below waterfalls or dams early and late in the year right into the fast water. Since these lures won't run too deep they are ideal to use under these conditions. Wobbling lures can also be used for "twitching" on the surface. Under certain conditions these plugs can be dynamite when walleye are feeding near the surface.

When fishing for suspended walleye, these lures are easy to run off of downriggers. When using downriggers to fish for these suspended fish, lighter cannonballs between five and seven pounds in weight should be used. The "lead" distance between the lure and the release on the cannonball or cable should be fairly long. Walleye can spook very easily and it is common to use a 10 to 30 foot lead. Walleye are usually light hitters, therefore, the release should go off with the slightest tug on the line.

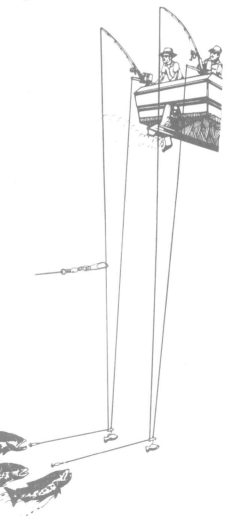

Crankbaits

These are the wobbling plugs that are the "counterparts" of the shallow running plugs. They can be made from the same materials and have very similar action, but the single most important difference is that the harder you "crank" the deeper these plugs will run. Most crankbaits usually have a heavier, bulkier appearance compared to the streamlined shallow-runners. Others like the Rapala Shad-Rap are very thin in appearance and they look identical to real baitfish. Because of their design and weight, they are ideal for casting. These lures are characterized by having long clear or solid lips which extend two to four inches past the plug. As soon as these plugs hit the water and you start to reel, they start to dive almost at 90 degrees toward the bottom. Most crankbaits will dive from seven to twenty feet.

As these plugs are being retrieved they will swim almost upright along the bottom. This makes them virtually snag-proof because the only thing that is bouncing along the bottom is the long lip. Some crankbaits are equipped with sound chambers which are good to use in murky, deep, or fast water, even at night.

The most popular crankbaits for walleye are; Rapala's Shad Rap, Rebels Deep Wee-R, Storm lures, Bomber baits, Bagley's Smallfry, Rebel lures, Arbogast's Mud-bug, Wally Diver and Rattl'in Spot.

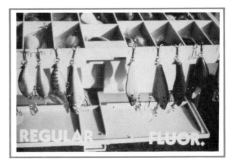

Crankbait Presentation

Crankbaits are ideal to use when trolling along deep structure or over deep weedbeds. As mentioned, their aero-dynamic shape and heavier weight make them ideal casting plugs when fished along shorelines, points, islands, weedbeds or even when casting from shore.

When you cast them out they don't have a lot of action on their own, however, they are designed to head straight for the bottom and that's where walleye are most of the time.

Jig Tactics

Jigs

This is probably the most versatile lure the walleye fisherman can stock-up on. More walleye are caught on various types of jigs across North America than any other "one" particular lure. Jigs are very simple lures. They have a weighted lead head and either a rubber or hair body.

Jigs come in a variety of shapes and sizes and are made from a variety of materials. It is very important to have a good assortment of these lures in your box. The most popular type of jig has a round head. These jigs can be purchased bare so that you can dress them with hair or a rubber body. Make sure if you plan to use a rubber action tail grub on the jig that it has a good "barb" on the shaft of the hook. This barb will help to keep the rubber grub on the jig longer and prevent walleye from tearing it off.

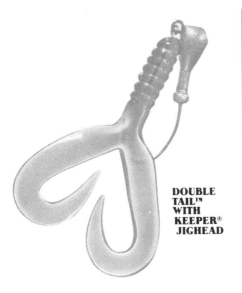

DOUBLE
TAIL™
WITH
KEEPER®
JIGHEAD

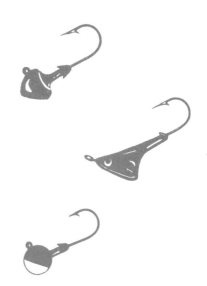

Round-headed jigs will fall fairly fast and put up low water resistance when being jigged along the bottom, or retrieved in a suspended water strike zone. "Power-head" jigs are ideal when fishing very rocky areas where you have the highest chances of getting "hung-up". "Slider-heads" are even more snagless and can be fished even in dense wood. The only problem in using these flatter-shaped jig heads is that they tend to drop very slow and put up a lot of resistance when you reel them in. "Banana" shaped jig heads are ideal when you need to cut through vegetation, or when one wants to fish deeper water with heavier weighted heads. Action tail grubs will work well when walleye are aggressively feeding. When they are "inactive", hair jigs can produce more fish. Some of the most popular jigs are; Marabou Feather jigs, Bucktail jigs, Tinsel Tail jigs, Vibrotails, Living rubber jigs, Tube jigs, Mister Twister jigs, Sassy Shad jigs, Beetle Spin jigs, Sting Ray grubs and Lindy's Fuzzy Grub jigs.

Jig Presentation

Jigs are the easiest lures to fish. All
you have to do is cast it out, let it hit
the bottom, lift it and let it hit the
bottom again. To become proficient in
fishing and all its specialized
techniques may take some time.

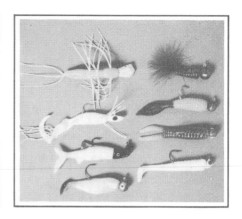

Jigs can be fished in many different
ways. Always make sure to tie a swivel
"in-line" about six to twelve inches
above your jig. This will make the jig
look natural, while at the same time
the swivel will absorb any line twist
that is created by the jig spiraling and
free-falling to the bottom. Jigs can be
vertically jigged in deeper water over
walleye holding structure. Best of all,

they can be cast and retrieved from
boat or shore.

They are ideal to use when drifting
with the wind over walleye areas or
trolled slowly along the bottom. They
can even be used as is, or for the
perfect tease, you can tip them with
live bait with almost no noticeable loss
of action.

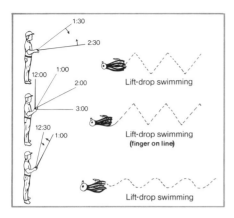

River fishermen know that the best lure they can use in fast water that will go to the bottom is a jig. Most fisherman who fish dams will cast their jigs upstream and retrieve it with the current ensuring that it will bounce along the bottom. Many people will anchor their boat in shallow water near weed beds or shallow-water structure and will cast and retrieve jigs. At times this is the only technique that will produce fish particularily when they are very spooky and you can't move around too much or troll. Heavy weed beds can be penetrated with jigs. "Rip-jigging" is the most effective way to fish a jig under these conditions, no other lure will take its place. Jig fishing requires the fisherman to always be ready to set the hook at the slightest tap, tug or change in the normal feel of the lure. Most of the time the only thing that is felt on the jig "take" is a slightly heavier weight, that's when it's time to "set the hook". Wherever you are fishing a jig, be it in shallow or deep water, it is most important to watch your rod tip to detect even the slightest movement. Remember, when jig fishing open water make sure you are using the lightest line possible because it will give you the most action from your jig.

Jigging Spoons

Many avid walleye fishermen have mastered various techniques with a variety of artificial lures but for some reason have ignored the simple "jigging spoon". Ice fishermen throughout Canada realize the effectiveness of jigging a spoon in one area when ice-fishing. These spoons are usually very simple looking. They are made out of lead or solid iron which is later plated and they are available in a variety of sizes ranging from 1/16 oz. to 8 oz. in weight. They are also inclined to be very productive because the action imitates an injured bait fish trying to dodge and dart away. Some of the most popular jigging spoons are; Swedish Pimple, Mr. Champ, Buzz-Bomb, Hopkins spoon, Rapala's Pilkie spoon and Johnson's Luhjon to name a few.

Presentation – Jigging spoons

These spoons can be fished close to the surface of the water over deeper weedbeds, or just under the surface by pumping and reeling the spoon back to the boat. These spoons have very erratic action and walleye usually can't resist them. The most popular method of fishing these spoons is vertical jigging in deeper water either for suspended walleye or for walleye that are holding very tight to structure. The fisherman usually tries to position his boat over the area he wants to fish then all he does is let line out until the spoon gets to the desired depth. The line is then reeled tight and the rod is moved up and then dropped letting the spoon "free-fall". It's usually at this time that the walleye will hit. Many walleye fishermen will add a trailer hook on these spoons and then will tip them with a minnow. This usually gets the most stubborn walleye to strike.

Spinner Tactics

Spinners

In many parts of Canada a spinner fished alone or tipped with a piece of worm is one of the deadliest lures you can use. Drift-fishermen have known for decades that by using a spinner under windy conditions they are adding vibration and flash to their bait thus catching fish consistently. Spinners can be cast and retrieved, trolled or even drifted with. These lures require minimum tension on the line to get them to work. For this reason they entice thousands of walleye to hit this lure every year.

Normal bladed spinners are designed for all-round fishing. The more tapered "willow" shaped bladed spinners will usually run deeper and are more desireable when you are moving at faster speeds. Some spinners come rigged with an added lead head to take the spinner down to deeper depths like the "Erie Dearie" models. These weighted spinners will work at various depths, but they are especially effective when trying to locate fish that could be suspended between ten to thirty feet down. Many bass fishermen have realized that "spinner baits" work extremely well for walleye in shallower weedy water. These tandem spinners are virtually snagproof and can be fished in the thickest weeds.

"The Whistler Concept"

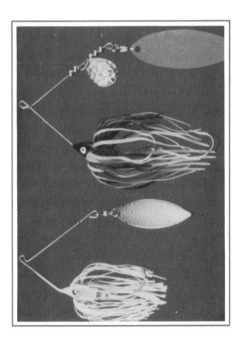

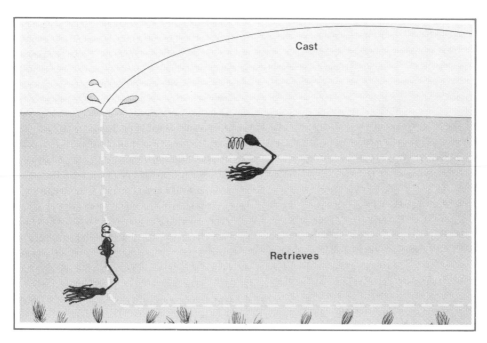

Cast

Retrieves

The most popular size of spinners to use when walleye fishing are between number 2 and 4. As far as weight is concerned 1/4 oz. to 3/4 oz. spinners work the best. Some of the most popular spinners for walleye are; Blue Fox Vibrax spinners, Blue Fox spinner baits, Erie Dearie spinners, Paul

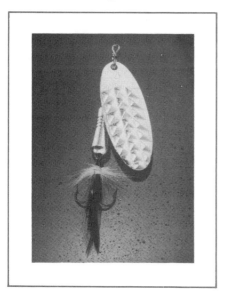

Bunyon spinners, Lusox spinner, Hildenbrandt Nugget tandem weighted spinners, Colorado spinners and Northland's Walleye Whistler.

Spinner Presentation

Whenever you are using a spinner, the most important thing to remember is to keep it as close to the bottom as possible. At times you may want to weigh down the spinner that you are using by adding split-shot somewhere up the line. Try casting spinners around weedbeds and along weedlines. Remember, whether spinners are visible to the eye or even if they are down deeper they'll give off maximum vibration and are ideal night time lures. Many times letting the blade of the spinner hit the bottom occasionally will trigger inactive walleye into striking. As a last resort when walleye may not want to co-operate, try tipping your spinner either with a worm or minnow.

Fly-Fishing Tactics

Flies

Throughout the season when walleye are found in shallower water they can be easily caught on a fly. Streamers are probably the most effective type of fly to use.

Some of the most popular flies are; Yellow Drake, Yellow Sally, Grey Ghost, Micky Fin and Marabou Muddler minnows.

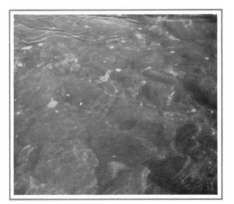

Presentation - Streamers

Use these early and late in the day when the walleye move over shoals, and shallow water structure or shallow weedbeds. It is very important to get your streamer as deep as possible which will mean using a weighted forward sinking fly line and heavier leader. Streamers are perfect baitfish imitation. No matter where you fish, always retrieve the streamer with a snapping, darting retrieve. This will resemble a crippled baitfish. If you plan on doing any fly-fishing at night, try using muddler minnow imitation streamers on the surface. Work the streamers across the top of the water giving them short jerks. You will be surprised at how hard walleye will take a fly off the surface.

Chapter 7

Live Bait

Live Bait

Live Bait/Types

There will be times throughout every season when the only way the angler will be able to catch walleye will be by using live bait. When there are drastic changes in weather, such as sudden "cold fronts" or many days of high pressure systems characterized by clear skies and temperate weather, walleye can become very "inactive". It seems that this is the time the serious walleye fishermen has to do everything he can to pamper the walleye into taking live bait. Just using live bait may not be enough. It is very important to present live bait in front of these walleye so that it is moving freely and so that the walleye has to make the least amount of effort to take the bait. This means using specific rigs and presentations that will put the bait "in front of their noses".

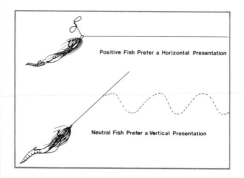

Positive Fish Prefer a Horizontal Presentation

Neutral Fish Prefer a Vertical Presentation

In the early chapters of this book we discussed the changing diets of maturing walleye. In this chapter we will be dealing with mature walleye and the types of baits they are most interested in.

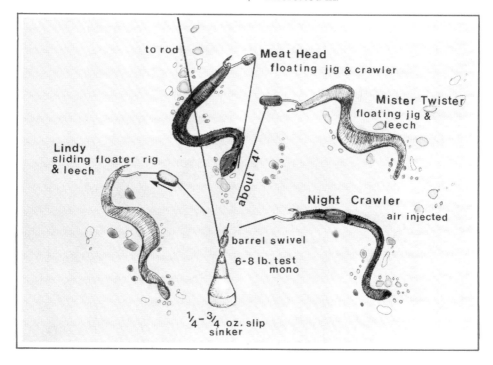

to rod

Meat Head
floating jig & crawler

Mister Twister
floating jig &
leech

Lindy
sliding floater rig
& leech

about 4'

Night Crawler
air injected

barrel swivel

6-8 lb. test
mono

$\frac{1}{4}$-$\frac{3}{4}$ oz. slip
sinker

The most popular live bait to use across Canada for walleye include; minnows, worms, leeches. Walleye can be caught on frogs, insects, larval grubs and salamanders. At certain times of the year one particular live bait will work much better than others. For example, early in the season walleye will be following schools of spawning baitfish throughout lake systems. Minnows would probably be top choice at this time of the year. When using minnows it is very important to fish with minnows that are native to the water you are fishing in. Some species of minnows are only found in fast-water areas and walleye that enter the river systems in the spring and fall become accustomed to feeding on these particular baitfish. Many live bait dealers will stock up on baitfish that are either very hardy or the most available at a particular season. The serious walleye fisherman should familiarize himself with the common baitfish found in the waters he fishes so that he can "match the batch".

Most live bait fishermen will start using worms and leeches as the season progresses into summer. Many fishermen have discovered that from mid-summer to late fall, frogs can be effective bait for walleye.

No matter which live bait you are using or at what time of the year, your bait should be fresh and lively. If walleye are really biting, they will take bait whether it is dead or alive, but as a rule a scrappy, struggling, fresh minnow or worm will catch more fish.

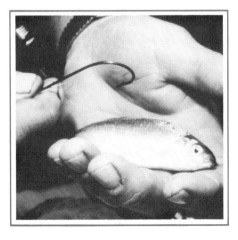

Live Bait Rigs

Many fishermen will head out on a lake and go to a nice weedy area where they know there are walleye. They will rig up their line with a hook and place a bell sinker, twist sinker or split shot somewhere above their hook, bait it with a worm, and cast it towards the weed bed.

That rig sinks to the weed-covered bottom and is motionless. As the angler brings in his rig he gets frustrated and moves on.

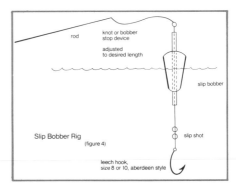

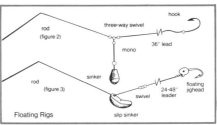

There are a variety of rigs that are designed for use under varying fishing conditions. These rigs work to make live bait look as real and natural as possible. If the fisherman in the above scenerio only knew about using a sliding bobber rig, or a floating jig head on a slip-sinker rig, he could have sat on his weed bed all day and had fun hooking walleye regularly, without getting any weeds on his bait. This is only one example of using a specific rig for a particular situation.

The most common rig for live bait fishing is a hook and sinker. This simple rig will work well when fishing open or fast water, that has few obstructions on the bottom to get

hung up on. It also works well when you are fishing live bait suspended from the bottom with your rod while laying it off the side of a boat or pier. A second popular live bait rig is to use the above rig and add a bobber to it. The bobber will suspend the bait at a specific height off the bottom. These two rigs are very basic and work well under limited conditions.

The next live bait rigs we will be discussing are more advanced and combine the latest "high-tech." terminal tackle. Across Canada, the sliding-sinker rig is probably the most versatile live bait rig you can use. A sliding sinker is threaded through the line. These sinkers can be of the bell, egg, or popular walking-type, that can be purchased for "Lindy Rigs".

Walking sinker
LINDY RIG

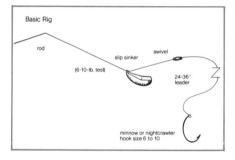

Basic Rig

rod

slip sinker

(6-10-lb. test)

swivel

24-36" leader

minnow or nightcrawler
hook size 6 to 10

Now that the sinker is free to move up and down the line, the angler has to place either a split shot, swivel, snap, or bead where he wants the sinker to stop. At this time he determines how long of a leader he wants in-between his sinker and hook. By using this rig the fisherman can apply any amount of weight he wants to keep his bait down. Once the walleye takes the bait, the line runs through the sinker and the walleye does not feel the extra weight. When using this rig it is important to always hook the bait at the head so that it is natural and streamline on the hook.

This is the explanation of the basic "sliding-sinker rig". Many anglers will make their baits buoyant with this rig by placing a small piece of foam right next to their hook, by using a floating jig head or by injecting their bait with air. This means that while the sinker is on the bottom, their bait can be suspended as much off bottom as the walleye fishermen desires by varying the length of the leader and the amount of buoyant material he uses.

When using these rigs it is most productive when you feel a hit, to let the walleye take the bait. This will ensure a good hook set. This rig works exceptionally well when used in combination with "back-trolling".

Snag – free in
most conditions

Another very popular bottom rig is a "bait-walker". A bait-walker is a sinker that is molded to a wire in the shape of a "V". One arm of the "V" has the sinker molded to it and lays on the bottom.

The other arm of the "V" has a leader attached to it and keeps the bait off the bottom. The fisherman attaches his line to the base of the "V" and when the rig is moving it bounces along the bottom and is virtually snagproof. This is an excellent rig to use when front trolling especially in deeper water and with adverse weather conditions. Again, the bait can be suspended in the same way as the "sliding-sinker rig".

Double-
Hook
Harness

INCREDIBLE
ON WALLEYE!

Slip-bobber fishing is very productive and convenient when fishing for walleye that are suspended in open water or over weed beds. To make a slip-bobber rig you have to use a float that permits the line to go through it. There are floats manufactured specifically for this type of rig. The main advantage to using this rig is that you can vary the depth of the float very easily and when you cast the float slides down to the sinkers to make casting easy. A small piece of "living rubber" material is tied to the fishing line. This "ball" of rubber will pass through your guides but will also act as the stopping point of your float. Therefore, if you want to fish your bait four feet down you place the small rubber stopper four feet up from the hook. The float would be sitting on the sinkers, but as soon as your rig would hit the water the float would let the line pass through it, until it reached the rubber stopper.

Another rig that has been made very popular in eastern Canada is a "pickerel-rig". This is a manufactured rig that is about fifteen inches in length. It has two "thin" wire arms that can rotate around the monofilament leader which is used to connect two snelled hooks to the line. This rig allows you to fish on bottom with two hooks, one above the other.

Many walleye fishermen who fish at night are not aware that they could be using a float that is very visible in the dark. Blue Fox Co. has a series of "light-floats" on the market that have been manufactured especially for use at night. They are powered by ultra-light "lithium" batteries that have the configuration and weight of a wooden match. These are excellent when night fishing for walleye with a suspended rig.

Using different colours of yarn tied just in front of the hook can be just as effective. Luhr Jensen plastic salmon eggs come in a variety of colours from red to fluorescent chartreuse. Even though these were developed for salmon and steelhead fishermen, they work extremely well as walleye bait "enhancers".

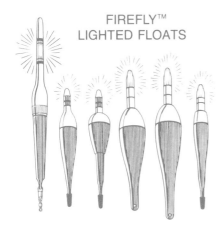

FIREFLY™
LIGHTED FLOATS

With all of the above rigs, attractors can be used in conjunction with the bait. Walleye fishermen for years have found that by using a small light-weight spinner in front of their hook, they could dramatically increase the number of strikes they would get.

Live Bait Presentation

Whenever you use the live bait bottom rigs, these rigs should be fished as close to the bottom as possible. These rigs are ideal for drift-fishing along breaks, weedbeds and weedlines. They are also extremely effective when used with "back-trolling" techniques.

The bobber techniques should be used whenever you are fishing for suspended schools of walleye in open water, or when fishing weed beds. It is possible to fish in between individual weeds by using the "slip-bobber" technique. The two most important points to remember when using these two techniques are:

1) Keep the bait as natural looking as possible, this means using minimum weight, the lightest line and avoiding steel leaders if possible.

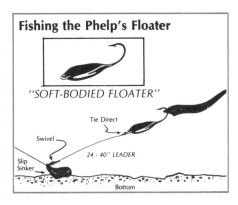

Fishing the Phelp's Floater

"SOFT-BODIED FLOATER"

Tie Direct

Swivel

24 - 40" LEADER

Slip Sinker

Bottom

2) Try to keep your bait in front of the walleye whether they are suspended or on bottom.

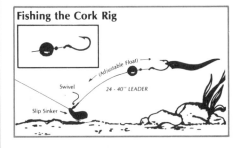

Fishing the Cork Rig

(Adjustable Float)

Swivel

24 - 40" LEADER

Slip Sinker

Live Bait Accessories

When using live bait it is very important to keep your bait fresh and lively. When fishing during hot weather periods and in bright sunlight this can be difficult. Minnows should be kept in metal, styrofoam or plastic minnow pails. Never overcrowd minnows in a pail they will soon start to run out of oxygen and will die quickly in a short period of time. If you have to go on long trips with live baitfish, keep them in an oxygen sealed bag with plenty of water.

Once you reach your fishing location place them in your minnow bucket and submerse them under water. In case of an emergency you should always have "oxygen tablets" with you for added protection. For walleye fishermen that do a lot of trolling with live minnows, they should consider purchasing a minnow bucket that is designed to be trolled along-side the boat.

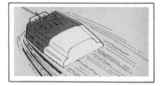

If you use a lot of worms, you should have a "worm box" at your home which will keep hundreds of worms healthy and ready for use. When taking fresh worms on a fishing trip they should be kept in a paper fiber-board or styrofoam box. Make sure the worms are cool and moist and they will remain fresh. The worst enemy of worms is dryness and heat. Leeches that you plan to keep for a day or two should be stored in an aerated container and the water should be changed regularly.

Chapter 8

Boats

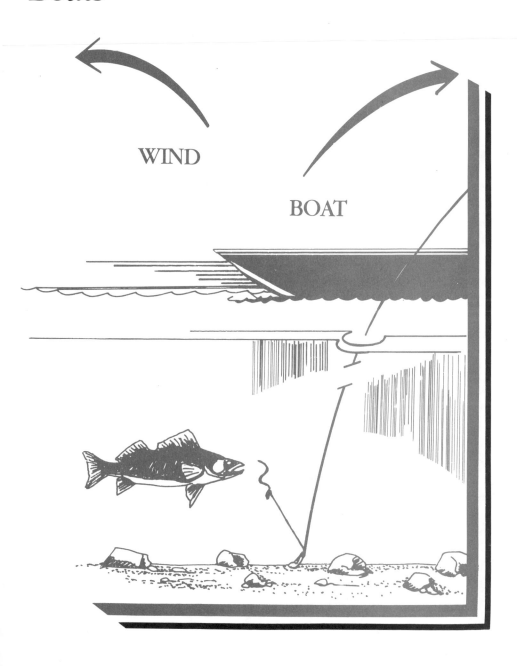

WIND

BOAT

Boats

Fiberglass & Aluminum

Walleye fishermen who take their sport seriously should consider investing their money in a boat that will help them specifically catch more fish. Most Canadian walleye fishing is done on big waters. This means using a boat that is between sixteen and eighteen feet in length. These boats can be made out of aluminum or fiberglass. Many walleye fishermen prefer to use aluminum boats because they are lighter, less expensive, easier to transport and easier to manually launch into a lake where there are poor or no launching facilities.

Outboards for these boats should be between 30 hp. and 60 hp. These motors will take you from spot to spot in a short period of time, so that you can maximize your fishing time. They will also allow you to troll between 4 and 6 miles per hour. For specialized Great Lakes walleye fishing, some fishermen will use large boats between 19 and 30 feet in length. Key factors to consider are seaworthiness, soft ride, cockpit space as well as good boat-handling characteristics.

A 14 foot aluminum boat powered by a 20 hp. engine is suitable for fishing smaller inland lakes. These type of boats account for many of the walleye that are caught across Canada each year.

Heavier fiberglass boats are more stable on the water and are less effected by strong winds. Many boat companies have been re-designing their fiberglass rigs to meet the walleye fisherman's needs. Fiberglass boats are usually much easier to control than aluminum boats. No matter what type of boat you have, your main concern should be "low end" speed.

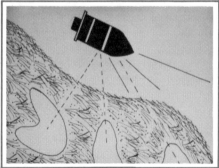

Walleye fishing is most productive when you move your boat at the slowest speed possible. This means an electric trolling motor is a MUST! Boats that will allow the fishermen to use a transom mount electric are best. Many walleye fishermen will have two electric trolling motors installed in their boat, one on the bow and one on the transom.

Serious walleye fishermen should consider driving by tiller handle rather than behind a steering wheel. Being on the motor will give you more precise control over speed and turning ability.

No matter how large a boat you own or are considering buying, it should be comfortable, stable, and deep. These features are essential so that you can navigate efficiently enough to maximize your fishing time, even under the worst conditions.

Fish finders on your boat are a must, especially if you plan to do any deep water fishing over 25 feet. If you plan to do a lot of trolling you should invest money in a couple of rod holders that clamp on to the side of the boat. If you use the "back-trolling" technique you should install "splash-boards" on the transom of the boat on either side of the outboard motor. Lighter aluminum boats will be better suited for extensive back-trolling because these boats will be more buoyant and will displace more water when trying to fish in adverse conditions.

"Low End" speed Trolling speed. Splash Boards Panels anchored to the transom of the boat extending ten to fourteen inches up from the transom. These boards are used to deflect water away from the transom of the boat when "back-trolling".

Chapter 9

Competitive Walleye Fishing

Competitive Walleye Fishing

Fishing derbies for walleye have been around for years, but since 1975 a new craze in competitive fishing has started in Ontario. The first annual Canada/U.S. Walleye Tournament was held on Pigeon Lake in Ontario. This set the standard for many walleye tournaments to follow.

For those of you that may not be familiar with these events, we will discuss the differences between walleye derbies and walleye tournaments.

Walleye Derbies

Derbies are usually several days to months in length. The entry fee for derbies is usually low, between five to fifteen dollars per person. There are very few restrictions to these derbies. They usually allow any type of bait to be used; you can catch your fish at anytime of the day or night; you can fish with other people from shore or from a boat and the fishing areas usually cover a small region. There are some special derbies that last only a few days and pertain to a certain lake, but these are only just starting to become popular in recent years. The goal for the entrants of these fish derbies is to catch the biggest fish. Usually the top five to ten heaviest fish win prizes. Usually a large percentage of all the money raised in these events goes to habitat improvement and re-stocking programs to perpetuate the fishery. Derbies usually are not promoted as catch and release.

Winning a derby usually takes a lot of luck. There are very few things a contestant can do to increase his odds of winning. In most derbies anglers fish individually and cannot have the help of other fellow fishermen. Derbies have become an important event in many communities throughout Canada, particularily to promote sportfishing and sportsmanship.

Walleye Buddy Tournaments

Walleye tournaments are very different from the derbies. They resemble the bass tournaments. Many of the contestants use fully equipped bass boats or "high tech." fishing boats with engines up to 150 h.p.. These tournaments are usually two days in

length, a Saturday and a Sunday. Competitors join together to form two man teams to compete against the rest of the field. Entries are anywhere from $100.00 to $200.00 per team and prizes are given as team prizes. Contestants usually must be over the age of twelve to be able to compete. There is usually one designated "Tournament Headquarters" that is used to start and finish each day's fishing. There are specific tournament boundaries and only certain waters can be fished during the tournament. Normal tournament fishing hours are on the Saturday from 7 a.m. to 4 p.m. and on the Sunday from 7 a.m. to 2:30 p.m.. All tournament entrants must wear lifejackets when operating their

motor boat. Boats are inspected each day prior to the start of fishing. There is usually a minimum size limit rule to qualify fish for weigh-in. Minimum size is usually fourteen inches (total length of fish). The object of these tournaments is to weigh in the six heaviest walleye a team is able to catch for the given day. At the end of the two days fishing the team with the heaviest weight for a two day limit, which would be a total of twelve walleye wins the tournament. Unlike the derbies, in these tournaments total overall weight wins. There usually is a prize given for the biggest fish caught on each of the two days, but these are usually nominal compared to the winner's purse. Normally a large percentage of the money raised in these tournaments goes back to be used for fisheries management and re-stocking programs.

Walleye tournaments are 100% live release. This means that each of the fish that is being weighed in has to be kept alive and in most cases "live-bait" is not allowed because it increases the chances of a fish swallowing the bait deep and then dying as a result. Competitors must use boats that are equipped with "live-wells". Once the fish are weighed they are released back into the lake and they must swim away.

If a team brings in dead fish they are given a penalty in the form of a loss in their overall weight.

These tournaments have become very popular in the last ten years because they promote sportsmanship, walleye fishing and catch-and-release which will ensure a healthy and on-going fishery for generations to come.

Some of the most popular tournaments are; The Canada/U.S. Walleye Tournament, The Labatt's North Bay Walleye Tournament, The Labatt's Lake St. Francis Walleye Championship and the Labatt's Stoney Lake Walleye Tournament.

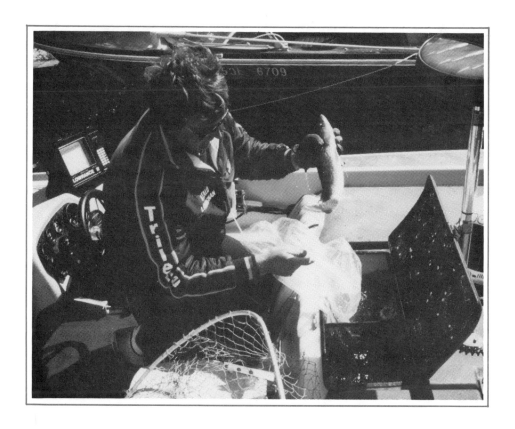

Chapter 10

Common Walleye Parasites, Diseases & Contaminants

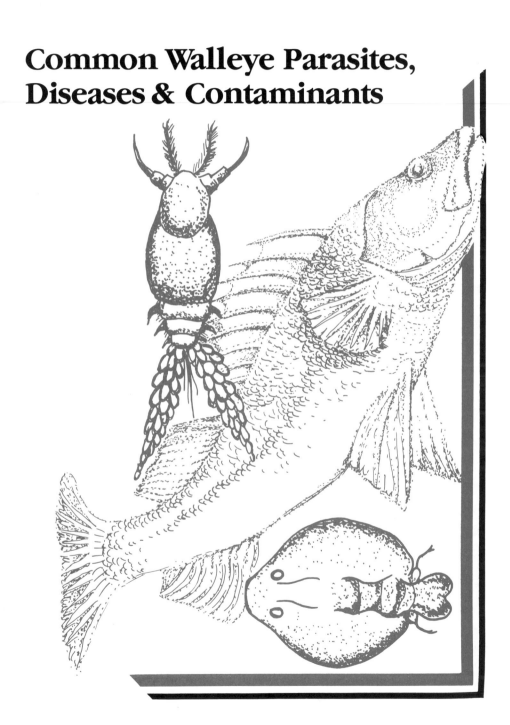

Common Walleye Parasites, Diseases & Contaminants

Parasites

In this chapter we will discuss the parasites, diseases and contaminants that may be commonly found in the walleye you are catching and eating.

Many of Canada's walleye, no matter where they are caught can be infested with some type of parasite, virus, bacteria or contaminant. We will start by discussing the diseases that can infect walleye in certain waters. In the second half of this chapter we will discuss contaminants.

One of the most disheartening experiences for an angler is to land a keeper or trophy walleye and discover it has black spots, warts, sores or wood on its body. You don't know whether to handle the fish, let it go, kill it, or take it home to eat.

Like all fish, walleye have to constantly fight off diseases. Many of these are caused by external factors; others are created internally in a fish. From the water surrounding them, the fish can become infected by bacteria, fungi, viruses and a variety of parasites which include worms, protozoans, crustaceans and lampreys. Other problems such as cancers, degeneration of certain organs, blindness and spinal abnormalities can arise from within the fish.

Like ulcers, degeneration of certain organs, blindness and spinal abnormalities can arise from within the fish.

Because there are so many different viruses, bacteria and parasites common to freshwater fishes, we will only be discussing those which are commonly found across Canada.

For those fishermen that may not know, a parasite is a small animal that lives inside or outside of another animal known as the "host". The parasite will draw body fluids and other nutrients from the fish without killing it. Each different species of fish has several kinds of parasites in its body. Fish parasites are common throughout Canada. Some parasites live in harmony inside a fish and they are not even noticeable. Other parasites can destroy a fish in a short period of time.

Different factors have a direct effect on the types and number of parasites that can infect walleye. For example, if fish are crowded in a body of water, the chances for parasite infestation will be greater. Older and larger walleye that eat smaller fish have much greater chances of becoming infected with parasites. During spawning, fish that receive external damage from scraping rocks become open to viral infections.

Let's start by discussing parasites that are found outside the body or on the gills of walleye.

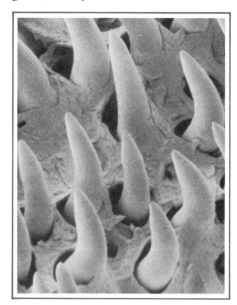

Lamprey

The lamprey is probably the most well known parasite that inhabits the Great Lakes watershed. The lamprey can be a deadly parasite. If one or more lampreys can anchor themselves to a fish for a long period of time, they can kill it. The lamprey has a large, round mouth which has a ring of sharp teeth. These teeth are used to attach itself to the surface of a fish. If the lamprey is able to penetrate through the flesh of the fish and reach the internal organs, the fish usually dies. The salmon and trout species get hit the hardest in the Great Lakes, but walleyes are attacked as well. Fish that survive lamprey attacks bear familiar circular scars usually on the sides of their bodies. These fish can be consumed. Most fisherman will cut away the area that has been marked by the lamprey.

Leeches

Leeches are usually found attached to the body of a fish. They can be found attached to the gills or inside the mouth. If enough leeches infest a fish, they can kill it. If fish have leeches attached to them when they are caught, the leeches can be removed and it is safe to eat the fish.

Lice and Fleas

Believe it or not, walleye can have lice and fleas. They are a lot different from those found on mammals, but they can do just as much damage. These parasites are part of the plankton that makes up a large diet of many smaller walleye. These lice and fleas will usually attach themselves to the fins and gills of their host. These parasites are usually harmless, but if a fish becomes infested, serious harm can be done. After cleaning these fish they are also safe to eat.

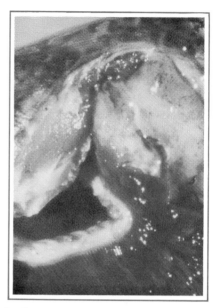

Black Spot

Flukes

Different species of flukes can infest gill areas on walleye. These are usually harmless unless they are found in great numbers. Flukes are most common on walleye which are caught in colder water. The fish affected by these parasites are safe to eat.

All of these external parasites can affect the fish , but they are harmless to human consumption and many anglers do not even know their fish contain some of these parasites.

Internal parasites are usually not seen unless a fisherman cleans his catch to eat it. Many fishermen do not eat fish that have external marking in the form of black spots. This is a very common parasite that is not harmful to man.

This parasite stage appears as small black specks on the skin of many fish. "Black Spots" are created when larval flukes penetrate the skin of a fish. Once the fluke is under the skin a cyst forms and it appears black on the surface. Many anglers refer to fish with "black spots" as being "wormy". They are partially correct, even though worms are not usually found in the fish, just the larval fluke. This is one of the most common parasites found in walleye across Canada. If the fish is well cooked, the meat is harmless.

Yellow Grub

This fluke is probably the second most common parasite found inside the walleye body in many of central Canada's lakes. A yellow cyst can be easily spotted in the flesh of a freshly cleaned fish. If the cyst is broken open, a small larval fluke about 1/4" long can be unraveled. These parasites do not do serious harm to the fish, but they are very unsightly to the fisherman planning to eat his catch. Cooking the fish flesh will kill this parasite, thus making them harmless, but most people can't bear the idea of eating worms with their fish. Yellow grub are commonly found in most of the warm water species of fish in Canada.

Tapeworms

Tapeworms are a common parasite found in walleye right across Canada. There are several different tapeworms which infest a variety of fish. Most of these worms are found in the fishes' intestines or in other parts of their bodies. Many walleye fishermen have probably experienced opening a plastic bag with their catch once they have arrived home and noticed these white strands covering their fish. Those strands are tapeworms which have left their host because it has died. Those types of tapeworms are harmless. One tapeworm can parasitize humans. This one exception occurs as a larval stage in the flesh of fish and develops into its adult stage in the intestine of mammals. The safest way to destroy tapeworms or any other internal parasite that you may not notice is to cook the meat thoroughly.

Fungus & Diseases

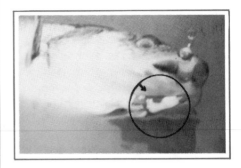

Fungus and diseases often develop with some walleye. Many fish that receive external injury or that are handled and released by fishermen are susceptible to fungus infection. Usually the growth of fungus starts as a small fuzzy speck on a piece of wood. If the fish lives in silty, mud bottom, the fungus can collect sediment from the bottom and can appear as a dark area on a fish. These fish can be eaten, but most anglers release these fish since their eating qualities are generally poorer than healthy fish.

Lympocystis

Lymphocystis is a virus-caused disease that is commonly found in walleye throughout Ontario and especially in the Bay of Quinte area. Lymphocystis will appear as an unsightly wart at times covering the bodies of some walleye. These warts appear to be harmless to the fish they develop on. There is no known way of controlling this virus. Fish with warts are safe to eat.

Most of the parasites that are found in walleye do not taint the flesh or make the flesh inedible by humans. Contaminants are invisible, and even though a fish looks perfectly healthy it could have toxic substances inside its fat and flesh.

Contaminants

In the first part of this chapter, we discussed the common parasites and diseases found in Canadian walleye. For the remaining of the chapter we will discuss the types of pollutants that exist across Canada and especially in the Great Lakes watershed of Ontario. We will discuss what these contaminants are, describe the effects these contaminants can have on human health, list the contaminants, inform you how they get into the water and the fish and explain why eating contaminated fish dramatically increases the volume of these toxic compounds entering our bodies. After reading this section you can decide whether or not you should be eating certain contaminated walleye.

In the last ten years, the government has tried to increase public awareness concerning contaminants in fish. The main problem, when it comes to educating the fisherman about contaminants, is to convince an angler that there is something wrong with a fish that looks perfectly healthy. To many fisherman, contaminants are an area which they know very little about. Most of the time, if a fisherman is told the fish he is eating may be poisoned, he may skeptically respond, "The fish fight hard, look fine and taste fine, c'mon, there's nothing wrong with them". There may indeed be something wrong with these fish and if consumed regularly they can effect human health.

Most of the time if a fish is infested by parasites or a disease, the parasites, welts and sores can be seen. Contaminants are absorbed in such tiny amounts by most gamefish, that even if they have high levels of these chemicals, there is no way of being able to detect these by the cosmetic appearance of the fish. Contaminants can be properly called "the invisible poisons".

Before we start talking about contaminants, it's important to understand why they exist. Some inorganic substances are naturally occurring in Canada, such as mercury.

Other inorganic and organic contaminants are man-made by-products that are a result of industry or products that are being used in agriculture to control weed growth and insect infestation which are dumped annually into rivers and lakes across the country.

Industrial and agricultural production has increased tremendously in Canada since the turn of the century, but the number of streams and lakes have remained the same. Thus, waste-water disposal problems are increasing every day. These "wastes" have a direct effect on aquatic vegetation, waterfowl and other water relating wildlife and ultimately the gamefish we are catching and eating.

Some of the words used in the rest of this chapter, because of their size, may scare you. When we tell you what some of these compounds can do to you it may not just catch your attention, but may also send chills up your spine.

Contaminants are toxic substances which in the last fifteen years have come to the attention of many scientists, biologists, conservationists and naturalists around the world. What are toxic substances? They are those compounds which, in sufficient amount on or in an organism can cause death, disease, mutation, deformity, or malfunction in that organism or its offspring. These include organochlorines, which are substances that are used as insecticides, pesticides, herbicides and in many industrial manufacturing applications. Several other organic substances and a list of toxic metals fall under this category.

Organochlorines are a group of toxic substances with known adverse effects on aquatic life and public health that have been identified in the Great Lakes watershed. Below is a chart listing a few of these substances and their description.

Toxic Substances

Name of Substance	Description/Use
Mirex (dodecachloro-pentacyclodecane)	Used as an insecticide and a fire retardant.
PCB'S	A family of chemically inert compounds, having the properties of low flammability, volatility and high dielectric constant. Used as hydraulic fluids, heat exchange and dielectric fluids, plasticizers for plastics, for pesticides and as an ingredient of caulking compounds, adhesives, paints, printing inks and carbonless copying paper.
DDT	A pesticide.
Heptachlor	An insecticide.
Endrin	An insecticide.
Aldrin/Dieldrin	Insecticides.

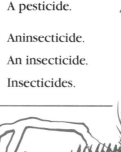

Below is a chart showing some of the other toxic organic substances with their descriptions.

Name of Substance	Description/Use
Toluene	Used in making dyes, pharmaceuticals and as a blending agent for gasoline.
Dioxin	A group of 75 chemicals of the chlorinated dioxin family.
Phthalate esters	Used in making dyes.
Furans	Used in the manufacture of nylon.
Styrenes	Used in making synthetic rubber, resins and plastics.

Toxic Organic Substances

Toxic metals is the last major group of contaminants. Some of these metals include arsenic, cadmium, chromium, copper, iron, lead, mercury, nickel, selenium and zinc.

All of these contaminants generally enter our lakes and rivers in five different ways.

1) Water discharge sites.
2) In the form of precipitation.
3) Sewage sludge.
4) Run-offs/groundwater.
5) Sediment deposits.

Different government groups have been monitoring the levels of these toxic compounds in fish throughout the country. In the last few years, test sites have been chosen at different points from coast to coast, including the Great Lakes watershed for periodic testing of a variety of pollutants. Tests and reports have established that there is a definite association between high contaminant levels in fish and large metropolitan cities that are heavily industrialized.

There are two frightening principles that fishermen should be aware of when dealing with human consumption of fish that have high contaminant levels.

1) The Principle of Biomagnification

The higher up the food chain contaminant consumption occurs, the higher the increase in contaminant concentration. To understand this, picture a baitfish eating plankton. The baitfish may contain .05 parts per million of a toxic substance in it's body. Let's use PCB's as an example. The acceptable level of PCB'c in Canadian gamefish which is considered safe is about 2.00 parts per million or less. Therefore, eating those baitfish would not be considered dangerous. A large 6-10 lb. walleye feeding on these baitfish may consume several hundreds of these baitfish in one season. It's contaminant level could realistically be as high as 20.00 parts per million. Now picture man ending the food chain and eating many of these walleye a year. Get the idea?

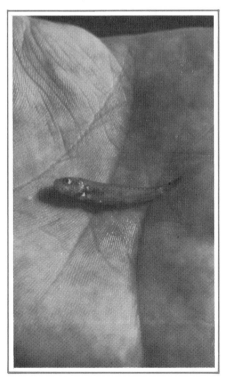

2) The Principle of Bioaccumulation

The higher the consumption of toxic substances, the higher the increase of concentration of these substances in living organisms. This means that those harmless parts per million of contaminants that are consumed over a long period of time will build up a volume of those substances that could become harmful in a living organism.

What does all this information mean? It means that it is a fact that there are gamefish in our Canadian waters that are contaminated with toxic substances. You can't see these poisons, but they are there. Certain large gamefish species caught from certain waters will have higher amounts of contaminant levels, than other smaller fish caught from different inland waters. If you fish for the fun of it and you release most of your fish, it won't matter where you fish or for which species. On the other hand, if you enjoy eating gamefish and you plan to eat your catch, make sure to choose waters that are "cleaner" than others to fish. Also, make it a rule to keep and eat smaller fish rather than the lunkers. Most of the contaminants found in many of the fish will be concentrated in the "fatty tissue" of the fish. As a precaution always remove the fat found along the back of a fish and around the belly area. Keep in mind these two very important principles when it comes to eating gamefish that may have levels of contaminants in them.

The Ontario Ministry of the Environment has documented information on lakes and rivers that have been tested for various toxic substances in the last few years. They have made this information available to the public free of charge. In Ontario these publications are called "A Guide to Eating Ontario Gamefish". There booklets are available from most sporting goods stores, LCBO outlets, the Ministry of Natural Resources offices or by writing to the Ontario Ministry of the Environment.

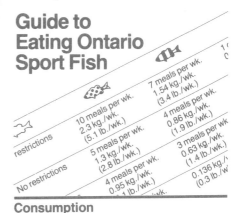

Guide to Eating Ontario Sport Fish

restrictions

No restrictions

10 meals per wk. 2.3 kg./wk. (5.1 lb./wk.)

5 meals per wk. 1.3 kg./wk. (2.8 lb./wk.)

4 meals per wk. 0.95 kg./wk. (2.1 lb./wk.)

7 meals per wk. 1.54 kg./wk. (3.4 lb./wk.)

4 meals per wk. 0.86 kg./wk. (1.9 lb./wk.)

3 meals per wk 0.63 kg./wk. (1.4 lb./wk.)

0.136 kg./w (0.3 lb./w

Consumption Guidelines

We hope that by reading this chapter your awareness has been increased in an area that few outdoor writers have chosen to explore. The increase of toxic contaminants in Canadian gamefish indicates that some waters are becoming more and more polluted. Today, many water systems are showing improvements in pollution control which directly decreases the level of contaminants in certain fish. Sportsmen across Canada have to become water conservationists, realizing that we don't have an unlimited amount of water at our disposal. The bodies of water we have been blessed with must be protected for multiple uses, including a healthy and thriving fishery. As sportsmen, we have a choice of having polluted, barren streams or those with clean water supporting healthy fish, waterfowl and other native wildlife. We believe that fishermen should be kept up-to-date and informed in all the various aspects of sportfishing, including any negative environmental conditions that effects our fishery. If anything, this chapter may have inspired you to have an active voice concerning developments that are directly effecting our sportfishery.

Chapter 11

Cleaning & Cooking Walleye

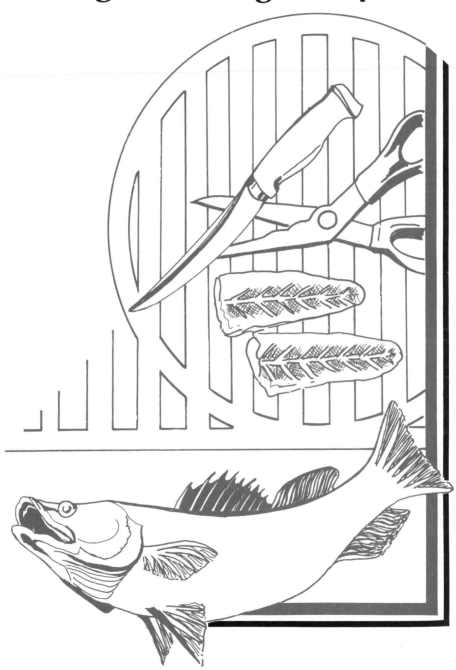

CLEANING & COOKING WALLEYE

Walleye are one of the easiest freshwater fish to clean. Most anglers will either cook the walleye whole, fillet it or cut it into steaks. The first thing the fisherman has to do before he can clean and cook his catch is to get it home as fresh as possible.

The possibility of fish becoming spoiled or tainted is affected by these three variables:

1) The handling and storage of the catch while fishing.
2) The way in which it is stored in your freezer or refrigerator.
3) The length of time it has defrosted before it is cooked.

As soon as a fish is landed, it should be handled and stored with special care until it reaches the kitchen. Many anglers use fish stringers or chains to hold their fish while they are fishing.

This system works fine under certain conditions such as fishing during colder weather or while fishing in colder water. Fish can be successfully kept on a stringer, but the stringer or chain should be long enough to allow the fish to swim in depths that are cooler than the surface water. Chains and stringers should be up to ten feet in length. During the hot summer months some lakes can reach surface temperatures of 80 F.. This means that the warm water will cause the fish to die and start to deteriorate immediately. If a fisherman is trolling most of the day and he is using a short stringer, the fish that are put on the

chain will die in a matter of minutes or hours. These fish that are dragged along the surface will go through algae, oil and at times even gasoline that can come off the engine. All of these things will detract from the wonderful flavour a fresh and well kept walleye can have.

The best way to keep walleye fresh immediately after they have been caught is to either use a live well, or cooler and ice to store them in.

Live wells that are properly aerated will eliminate the problems that you can have when you try to keep fish alive on a stringer. Water in the live well should be circulated and changed regularly. Most fisherman that have live wells can keep their catch alive until they reach home and are ready to clean it.

The safest and easiest way to ensure your catch will be fresh until you get it home, is to store it in a cooler with ice. On every fishing trip, the fisherman should take some plastic bags, block or cube ice, a large capacity cooler and his fillet knife with him so that he is ready to do the job properly. For best results, kill your catch right after you land it. Gut and clean your catch on the spot. Place the whole clean fish or fillets in a plastic bag and place them in between the ice chunks or cubes in the cooler.

If you are fishing in a back lake or are a long distance from any ice or cold storage, you must give your catch special attention if you want to get it home fresh. Under these circumstances, try to keep your catch alive as long as possible. When you are ready to leave, clean the fish and wrap it with a wet cloth or paper towels. Do not place the fish in a plastic bag when you are transporting it for any length of time in a vehicle. The plastic bag will raise the air temperature inside and will cause the fish to deteriorate very rapidly. Place the fish in a cardboard box and keep it somewhere where there is air circulation to keep it cool. Do not put the fish in the trunk of the car. Your catch should remain cool and fresh until you get it home.

Coolers such as the ones available from Coleman will keep your catch cool for more than 24 hours. Of course, block ice will last longer, but it does not give the same cold temperature distribution found in the cooler.

When freezing fish for longer periods of time, make sure the clean pieces of fish are drip dried before they are wrapped and frozen. Freezer quality wax paper should be used to initially wrap the fish. Next the fish should be placed in an air tight thick plastic bag, then frozen. You can double wrap your fish fillets for maximum freezer protection. Make sure you label all your catch with contents, weight, date the fish were caught and the freezing date. By following these steps you can insure your walleye will stay flavourful for up to nine months. Now you'll have in your freezer fresh flavorful walleye ready for immediate cooking, or for future gourmet meals.

Once the fish reaches home, the angler can do one of two things, eat the fish fresh within a day or two or freeze it to enjoy at a later date. Fish that are eaten the same day they are caught will have the most flavour. If plans are made to eat the fish within a few days, the clean fish can be successfully kept in the refrigerator. The clean fish should be placed on some serviettes or paper towels on a plate. Daily the fish should be checked and any moisture picked up by the absorbent paper should be wrung out. Fish can be kept fresh for one to three days in the refrigerator. If you are going to keep fish in the refrigerator we advise that you decrease the temperature to just below the freezing point.

Many people allow fish to defrost for too long a time. Fish flesh starts to deteriorate the minute it starts to un-thaw. Have you ever wondered why the cooking instructions on store bought frozen fish recommend that you cook the fish frozen? It's because they want your purchased frozen fish to taste as good as possible. More importantly, defrost your fish quickly. Once the fish starts to reach room temperature you should be starting your recipe preparations.

Cleaning Fish Whole

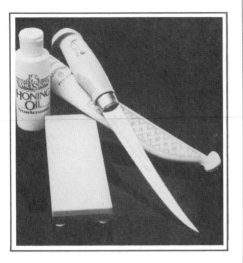

If you plan to keep your fish whole the procedure for cleaning the fish is very easy. Some fishermen enjoy eating the skin of their fish, therefore start by scaling the fish. Next, remove all fins from the body. This is done by inserting a sharp knife along the dorsal spine and cutting just below the skin on either side of the dorsal ray, then pulling this fin out. The procedure is repeated on the rest of the fins. Next, make an incision in the back of the fish where the head connects to the body. The cut should go down far enough so that the backbone is broken and the head is separated from the main body. At this time pull the head off at the same time removing the intestines and other internal organs. Rinse the fish, remove the blood line found along the backbone and it is ready to freeze or to cook whole.

Filleting Walleye

There are several methods of filleting a walleye. We will discuss the method that we find most practical and that we use most often.

Lay the fish on its side. Start by inserting the knife at the base of the head where it meets the back. Pass the knife horizontally so that it comes out at the belly on the opposite side of the fish. Very carefully work the knife back to the tail, cutting around the rib cage and making sure you do not go into the body cavity.

Once you have removed one side, you repeat the procedure on the other side. When you have both fillets with the skin attached it is time to remove the skin. Place the fillet skin down on a surface, hold the skin at the tail end of the fillet with your fingers, insert the knife at the base of the tail and work it along the skin towards the front of the fillet. This technique will cleanly separate the flesh from the skin and will give you a clean fillet. The fillet is now ready to be rinsed off then cooked or packaged for freezing.

Steaking

For the fishermen who enjoy fried walleye pieces and steaks and don't mind cleaning bones, just clean the fish whole as explained above and then cut the fish into chunks or steaks. Remember when cleaning walleye that the cheek meat is very muscular and is considered a delicacy by many fish connoisseurs.

Recipes

Here are some recipes to spice up your walleye. Most fisherman will agree that walleye taste so good that you can bake them or fry them without any extras and they still taste delicious. We believe that variety is the spice of life! Try these recipes and "Bon appetite"!

Walleye Fingers

1 ½ lb. of walleye fillets
1 cup buttermilk
1 cup yellow corn meal
flour
salt and pepper
corn oil

Cut the fillets into narrow strips about ½″ thick as well as ½″ wide. Season to taste. Dip in buttermilk and roll in corn meal mixed with a small amount of flour. Place in very hot corn oil (about 475 degrees F.). Fry until golden brown. Drain and serve immediately with tartar sauce.

Smokin' walleye

1 ½-2 lbs. walleye fillets

¼ cup soy sauce
2 tablespoons cooking oil
½ tablespoons, liquid smoke
1 garlic clove, minced
¼ teaspoon ground ginger
2 tablespoons butter

Mix soy sauce, oil, garlic, smoke and ginger then spoon over walleye fillets. Allow fillets to marinate 15 minutes, turning once. Place fillets on grill over moderately hot coals. Grill for 3 minutes each side until fillets flake when probed with a fork. Place a dab of butter on each side of fillet when served. Serves four.

Ontario's walleye chowder

1 lb. walleye fillets, 1 ½″ chunks
½ cup diced onion
½ cup diced celery
¼ cup diced green pepper
¼ cup butter
2 cups water
2 cups chopped tomatoes
1-12 oz. can tomato juice
herbs
3 parsley sprigs
2 garlic cloves, halved
½ teaspoon dried thyme
2 cups diced raw potatoes
dash of tabasco sauce
paprika
salt and pepper to taste

Sauté onion, celery and green pepper in butter until tender. Add water, tomatoes, tomato juice and herbs. Cover and boil for 15 minutes. Add potatoes, tabasco, salt and pepper to taste. Simmer for 30 minutes. Add fish and cook another 10 minutes. Sprinkle with paprika and serve. Makes four to six servings.

Beer batter walleye

1 ½ lb. thin walleye fillets
lemon juice
seasoned flour
¼ cup cooking oil
batter:
  ¾ cup flour
  ¼ teaspoon salt
dash of pepper
¾ cup beer

Cut fillets into 2″ strips. Sprinkle with lemon juice and roll in seasoned flour. Mix batter by blending beer into ¾ cup of flour with salt and pepper. Heat oil in heavy skillet. Dip each fillet in batter and fry quickly in hot oil about 2 minutes on each side. Check fish for flakiness by probing with a fork. Drain on paper toweling and serve with tartar sauce. Serves four.

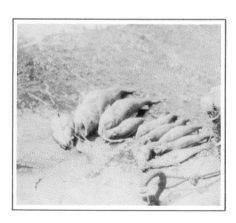

Campside walleye

2 walleye (14″) 16″)
6 tablespoons butter
4 tablespoons olive oil
flour, salt and pepper
2 eggs beaten
2 cups finely crushed corn flakes.

Fillet walleye and dry them thoroughly on paper toweling. Dust with seasoned (salt and pepper) flour. Dip fish in egg and roll in corn flakes. Heat butter and oil in heavy skillet. When pan is sizzling hot, add the walleye. Brown for 4 minutes on each side. Cover the pan, reduce heat to medium and continue cooking for 3 more minutes. Check fish at thickest place with a fork. If flesh flakes, it is done. Serves six.

Poor-man's shrimp (walleye shrimp)

Salt and pepper
Bay leaves
2 lb. walleye fillets

Cut the walleye fillets into strips ½″ thick, 1″ wide and 4″ long. Boil water add salt and bay leaves. When water reaches boiling point drop in the walleye strips. Let boil for precisely 1 minute. Remove fish pieces, drain and rinse immediately with cold water. Place curled up walleye strips in refrigerator and let cool. Serve with tartar or seafood sauce. Tastes just like shrimp.

Chapter 12

Conservation

Conservation

Walleye Conservation

The walleye populations that we have across Canada are native to our country, unlike many species of fish that have been introduced into our provinces. We can be proud of this fish.

It is very important for fishermen to be conservationists and realize the effect that over-harvesting can have on a given population. Years ago, to be a good fishermen a person had to consistently bring home his limit. This concept is contrary to the sportfishing ideals which we have today. It is common to look back at old pictures and see a party of fishermen all holding up one or more limits of walleye. Today, this type of harvesting cannot be tolerated by lakes and rivers located within driving distance of major urban areas.

Catch & Release

Educated fishermen realize that it is fine to keep fish to eat. Walleye are some of the best eating fish available in Canada and it's therefore important to release more fish then the ones they plan to keep. There is a motto that is popular around the lakes and rivers across Canada, "limit your kill – don't kill your limit" and it is true! If we love this fishery and want to see it become more abundant so that it exists for generations to come then we must practice "Catch and Release" methods.

In many parts of this country walleye populations are drastically altered because man diverts rivers or controls heights of water systems. This usually results in the destruction of spawning grounds or the killing of fertilized eggs that are ready to hatch.

Fast water areas in different provinces have been created to form new spawning grounds for walleye. Known spawning grounds are protected and monitored so that spawning walleye can successfully complete their spawning cycle.

Fish sanctuaries have been established below dams, at waterfalls and along causeways, where walleye tend to be most concentrated during the spawning season. Fishing seasons for walleye have been regulated in many parts of Canada, so that areas that hold late spawners have extended closed seasons and early closing seasons in the fall.

Size restrictions have been placed in many lakes where walleye populations are trying to establish themselves. In certain waters, the legal limit has been reduced from 6 fish to 4. All these elements have been created to help our walleye fishery and keep it from diminishing. If more anglers would use proper catch and release methods, fish populations would increase and the quality of sportfishing would be better. Three main factors affect the survival of walleye when catch and release methods are being employed after a fish had been landed:

a) How the fish is handled.

b) Where it has been hooked.

c) How long it has been kept out of the water.

The obvious answers are to handle your catch as little as possible. Try not to let the fish flop around on the bottom of the boat or on the ground. Never use your feet or hands to "jam" the fish against any rough surface. Remember that whenever something rough and dry comes in contact with the fishes skin, the fish will lose its protective slime covering in that area. If it loses its slime, the fish will be open to infections and disease. When handling fish that will be released, always make sure your hands are wet, not dry. Here's three easy steps when handling fish that will be released.

1) Try to hold the fish securely in one spot, preferably just behind the gills on the main body.

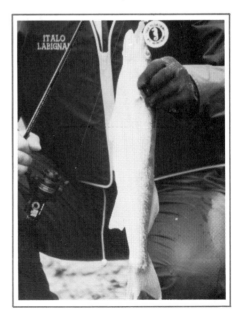

2) Remove the hook with needle-nose pliers to save time (barbless hooks will help here).

3) If possible, try to keep the walleye in the water during these procedures.

Walleye are not too difficult to handle when they are held with a firm grip. We have been using Normark's filler glove to securely hold the fish. In fact, we feel that these gloves are better than a net. Many times when a fish is netted , it will thrash in the net. This causes the fins and tail to split which exposes unprotected tissue leaving it open to infection.

Most of the time walleye are hooked very lightly through the skin along their jaws or just inside the mouth. There are of course times when walleye are hooked deep. Two things can be done under these circumstances: the hook can be left in the fish, which means the angler cuts his line or the fish should be kept and killed. Many times anglers try to remove hooks that have been swallowed deep. This usually does more harm than good. A hook that is left in a fish will usually disintegrate in time or will eventually fall out. Sometimes walleye are foul-hooked.

For example, walleye often will be finicky in their eating habits and will strike a bait too slowly or too quickly causing themselves to get foul-hooked by the angler. These fish that receive cuts or wounds on their bodies should also be kept. With increasing catches year after year due to the addition of advanced fishing electronics, equipment and tackle, sportfishing for walleye will suffer greatly if most of the fish are not released.

Walleye Stocking Programmes

In many parts of Canada, the government has established fish hatcheries that produce hundreds of thousands of walleye fry each season. These fish are usually released into new lakes which have favourable conditions to maintain walleye populations, or in lakes that receive heavy fishing pressure from cottagers and nearby cities. In many lake systems, predatory fish such as the muskie and northern pike are so plentiful that if there is a lack of smaller coarse fish in that particular lake, they will readily feed on young walleye. In these cases re-stocking programs are very valuable.

Conservation Organizations

There are many conservation organizations from coast to coast. For example, in Ontario, the largest is the Ontario Federation of Anglers and Hunters (O.F.A.H.) These type of non profit, non-government organizations are constantly involved in research, habitat rehabilitation, as well as educational programs. When we talk about education, we are talking to both the young and old alike. The most important group however, is the young of tomorrow. Many conservation organizations stress the study of ecology, angling techniques and live release. These are valuable tools for tomorrow's fishermen.

Remember, conserve our waters and from both of us Good Fishing!

Glossary

GLOSSARY

ALGAE BLOOM – When water conditions are suitable, small living organisms in the water known as plankton will re-produce very rapidly. Normal water colour will change to shades of green and in some lakes the water will resemble the consistency of pea soup.

AMBUSH – The act of lying in wait for or of attacking by surprise from a concealed position.

AMPHIBIANS – One of a class of vertebrates characterized by a three chambered heart, cold-bloodedness and skin lacking hair, scales or feathers. Many species hatch and develop in water. In their aquatic stage they use gills for breathing. Later, they develop lungs and spend part of their adult lives on land. Example: frogs and salamanders.

BACKTROLLING – A popular technique to use when fishing for walleye. The engine is placed in reverse gear and the angler trolls backwardly. This technique gives the angler total control over his speed and maneuvers.

BACKWASH – An area created when fast-water meets slow water and the direction of flow reverses itself. Backwashes are common in rivers and streams below waterfalls, dams and in large pools.

BAITCASTING – This term refers to any rods that have pistol grips or trigger grips which are designed to be used with baitcasting reels. These reels will have a level-wind or center-wind line pick-up mechanism and are designed to be operated with the thumb and hand when casting.

BAITFISH – Minnows, alewife, freshwater herring and smelt are common baitfish eaten by walleye.

BEND – This term refers to the bend in a river, where the river makes a directional turn and current is channeled and increased. Bends usually have deeper water and undercut banks.

BLANK CONSTRUCTION – This term is used to described the manner in which the rod blank is manufactured. The material that is used to form the blank can be rolled with the fibers going in various directions. Standard blank construction is linear, radial or woven.

BOTTOM FEEDERS – This term refers to the feeding behavior used by a mature walleye. Walleye will do most of their feeding on or near the bottom of the lake.

BOTTOM-WALKING WEIGHTS – Fishing weights that have a wire frame in a "V" configuration with a banana shaped sinker molded on one end. These sinkers are designed to bump along the bottom and are as snagproof as can be.

BREAK UP – A time period when the ice covering a lake starts to separate and sink into the warmer water below.

COARSE FISH – Most warm-water fish that are not considered gamefish are commonly called coarse fish. These include: suckers, carp, catfish and various species of panfish.

COLD FRONT – Sudden drops in temperature of ten degrees or more after a stretch of moderate to warm temperatures would be considered a "cold front". Some cold fronts last a matter of hours, some last for days. Cold fronts are usually produced by a high pressure system suddenly moving in on a low pressure system.

CONTROLLED DRIFTING – Drifting with the use of an anchor, sea anchor, electric trolling motor or outboard engine in such a way, so that the fisherman is controlling the direction and speed he is drifting at.

CONTROLLED TROLLING – Trolling with the use of an electric trolling motor or outboard engine in such a way, so that the fisherman has total control over the direction and speed he is trolling at.

COOL WATER – Walleye cannot tolerate constant water temperatures over 80 degree fahrenheit. Maximum high, cold water temperatures would generally not exceed 75 degrees.

"COUNT-DOWN" RAPALA – A weighted wobbling lure that has been designed to be used with a "count-down" technique. The fisherman casts the lure and when it hits the water he starts counting as it drops. This method is mostly used when trying to locate suspended fish.

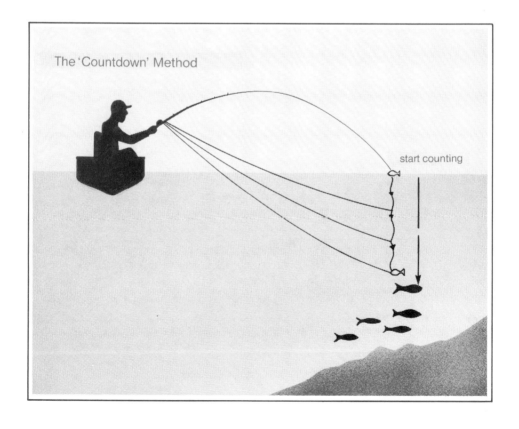

The 'Countdown' Method

start counting

COVER – Something that protects, shelters or guards. A place of natural shelter for a fish to hide for security or as a place of ambush. Cover can be made of rocks, wood, weeds and even surface turbulence.

CRANK – This term describes the technique used to retrieve a deep diving or shallow running plug. The angler has to continuously "crank" or reel-in the lure to give it proper action.

CRUSTACEANS – A description which includes a large class of Arthropoda made up of freshwater arthropods, such as water flies, freshwater shrimp and crayfish. These aquatic creatures have segmented bodies with a firm exoskeleton, walking legs and swimmerets.

CURRENT BREAK – An area in the water where fast flowing water meets slow moving or still water. Current breaks are usually produced when bottom structure protrudes up from the bottom or where other obstructions force the current in a certain direction. High winds and seiche movement in a lake can produce currents and current breaks.

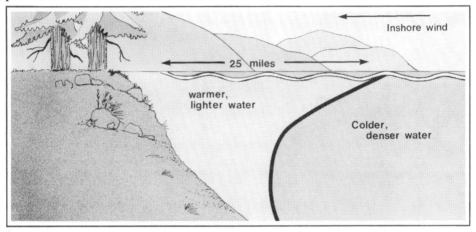

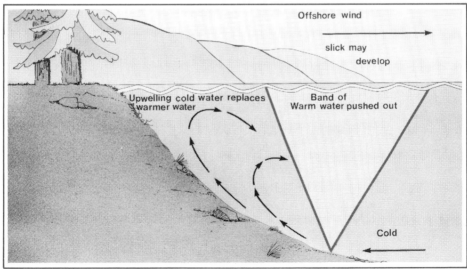

DEEP CRANKING STICK – These rods are usually seven to eight feet in length, they have a long butt and are equipped with a "trigger" reel seat. The action of these rods is usually very stiff.

DOWNRIGGER – A mechanism that consists of an flexible arm, a large reel, a lead cannon ball and wire line that is used to deliver a fisherman's line and lure to a desired depth.

DOWNRIGGER FISHING – A fishing technique in which a downrigger is used in conjunction with a cannon ball, wire line and a release to deliver the fisherman's bait to a desired depth.

DRESSED JIG – A jig that either has hair or bucktail tied to it, or that is used with a rubber grub body.

DRIFTING – A boat-fishing technique used to catch walleye in which a fisherman lets his baited line out and lets the wind push the boat so that his bait drifts through the water.

DROP-OFF – An area of underwater structure where the bottom increases in depth five feet or more in less than a three foot distance.

EUTROPHIC – A lake rich in dissolved nutrients, shallow and with seasonal oxygen deficiency in the hypolimnion.

FALL TURNOVER – An occurrence in a lake when the surface water becomes colder then the warmer water below and because of it's higher density, the colder water drops and mixes with the warmer water. This usually happens across Canada between October and November prior to "ice-up".

FIRST ICE – The time period when a lake newly freezes over and makes enough ice so that it is safe for fishermen to venture onto the ice for the first time.

FLASHER – This is a type of fish finder. A flasher gets it's name from the way in which it relays information to the angler. Depth readings and fish are recorded as light flashes on a screen.

FLAT – A feature in a lake or river where the bottom is shallower and even in depth than the surrounding water. Flats are usually created when sediments, such as soil, silt or other deposits, build up in a given area. Strong winds and current action account for most of the flats existing in a given body of water; therefore, flats are usually located near river channels, river mouths and wind-blown ends of lakes.

FLIPPING – A fishing technique developed for catching largemouth bass. The angler drops or "flips" his bait along undercut banks, holes in weedbeds and along weed edges.

FLIPPING RODS – These rods are usually seven and one half to eight feet long, they have a long butt, they are equipped with a "trigger" reel seat and they are designated as "heavy-action" rods to be used with 20 – 40 lb. test line. These rods are usually semi-telescopic, allowing the main part of the rod blank to collapse into the lower part of the rod blank near the reel seat and butt area.

FLOAT RIG – A technique where a buoyant float is used above the bait to keep the bait suspended off the bottom.

FLOATING JIG HEAD – A jig head that is made out of a buoyant material such as cork or foam. These types of jigs will suspend live bait off the bottom.

FOOD SHELVE – An area in a lake or river where there is a rich nutrient supply that stimulates fish and plant growth.

FORAGE – A general term used to describe the food consumed by fish.

FREE-SPOOLING – This term is used to describe a procedure that occurs when an angler using a baitcasting reel wants to let line get of the reel . When a person casts with a baitcasting reel he engages a release mechanism which allows the spool to roll freely permitting the line to go out.

FRONT TROLLING – This is the standard trolling technique. While the boat is moving in a forward position, the angler lets his line out so that the boat will pull the bait through the water.

GREY LINE – This is a feature that can be found on liquid crystal and paper recorders. The grey line feature allows the person operating the fish finder to make the bottom reading appear as a thin line rather as a dark band.

HABITAT – The natural living place of an animal or plant.

HARDPAN – The original layers of clay, cemented materials and main rocks and boulders that make up the bottom of a river or stream.

HEAD – This term specifies a location on a stream or river. The head area of a river is located at the beginning of a pool where the rapids change to flowing deeper water.

HEAVY ACTION – This term refers to the stiffness of a fishing rod. Fishing rods that are designed to be used with fifteen to 30 lb. test line and with lures weighing between 1/4 and 1 1/2 oz. are classified as heavy action.

HOLES – These areas can be found in rivers or lakes. Holes is the general term used to describe the deepest areas in a body of water.

HOT-FRONT – This usually occurs when a warm pressure system moves into an area that has had generally cold weather for a number of days. A hot-front is usually characterized by a temperature increase of ten degrees or more.

HOT-SPOT – A general term used to describe an area in a river, stream or lake where is a concentration of fish that can be readily caught.

ICE-OUT – This term describes a period of time when the ice that covers a frozen lake melts or is blown along the shoreline creating open-water.

INACTIVE – This is the term used to describe a phase when fish are in a negative mood. At this time they will be stationary and will be located suspended or close to the bottom of a given body of water. These fish will usually not move to strike a bait and so are extremely hard to catch.

INVERTEBRATES – Any animal that does not have an internal backbone, such as protozoa, shellfish and insects.

LATERAL LINE – A longitudinal line along each side of the body of most fishes that is usually distinguished by dash-like marks or differently coloured scales. The lateral line contains the openings of the lateral line organ which a fish uses to detect vibrations.

FISH FINDER – A type of electronic equipment that enables a fisherman to record the presence of fish in the water below the boat. A transducer and a receiver with a screen are the two main components to a fish finder. Most fish finders require a 12 volt battery as their power source.

LEAD – This is the line distance in between a cannonball and the fisherman's lure.

LIGHT ACTION – Light action is used to define rods that are designed to be used with four to eight lb. test line and with lures weighing from 1/8 to 1/4 oz.

LINE DIAMETER – This expression describes the thickness of the outside surface of any fishing line. Line diameter is usually measured in thousands of an inch.

LIQUID CRYSTAL RECORDER – This is a type of fish finder. The screen of these units give the fisherman a picture that is created on a liquid crystal medium.

LIVE BAIT RIGS – These rigs are made up of a piece of monofilament line to act as a leader, a single bait holding hook and a sliding sinker. These rigs are designed to be used with live bait that can be fished on the bottom or suspended off the bottom with the use of flotation device attached near the hook.

LOCALIZED – Localized populations of walleye will remain in a general part of the lake. These fish will migrate within this area and will seldom leave it.

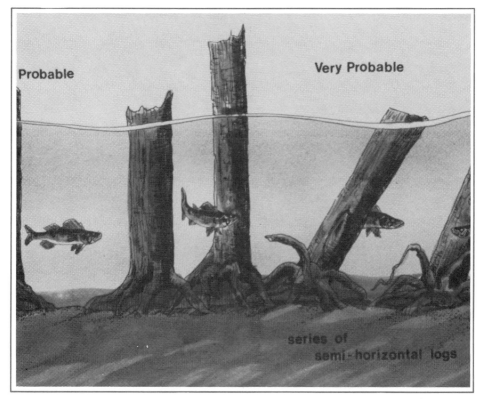

"LOW END" SPEED – Trolling speed.

MAGNETIC BAITCASTERS – These baitcasting reels are equipped with magnets that can be used to slow down the spool using gravity friction when the reels are "free-spooling".

MEDIUM ACTION – This term describes rods that are designed to be used with ten to fourteen lb. test line and with lures weighing 1/4 to 1/2 oz. in weight.

MEZO – This is the term used to describe a lake that shows eutrophic and oligotrophic characteristics.

MID-DEPTH FEEDERS – A feeding stage of walleye where these fish feed on suspended aquatic organisms and small fish in between the bottom of the lake and the surface.

MIGRATE – The act of moving at regular periods of time from one location to another.

NATURAL BARRIERS – Waterfalls, very fast rapids and shallow seasonal streams that connect lakes are examples of natural barriers that stop walleye migration.

NEUTRAL – A phase fish are in when they can be induced to strike. When fish are "neutral", they will move to attack a bait.

NOODLE RODS – These rods are normally twelve to fourteen feet in length and have a very light action. They are designed to be used with very light line between two and four lb. test.

OLIGOTROPHIC – This term describes lakes that have a deficiency in plant nutrients, an abundance of dissolved oxygen and no stratification.

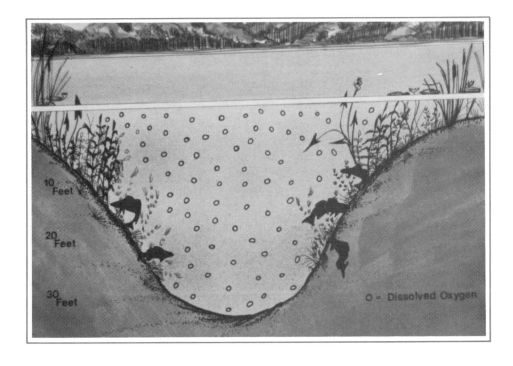

ONE-PIECE CONSTRUCTION – All rods that are not collapsible and that do not come apart fall under this category.

PAPER RECORDER – This is another type of fish finder. Most paper recorders are computer programmed. These units give the fisherman a printed paper display. The information recorded is permanent and can be kept and used for future reference.

PATTERN FISHING – Pattern fishing is looking for similar water conditions with certain common elements that have produced fish under identical conditions at different locations on a given body of water.

PATTERNS – A combination of tactics and locations on a lake which a fisherman establishes that consistently produces fish. A log will help you to easily identify your recorded data and in turn construct a plan of attack including things like proper tackle, presentation, fishing structure and much, much, more.

TIME	AM	PM	SPECIES; LURE PARTICULARS; BOTTOM AND
CAUGHT			STRUCTURE DESCRIPTION; RIVER/LAKE LOCATION
LENGTH	"	CM	SPECIES:
WEIGHT	LB	OZ	LURE:
		KG	MODEL:
DEPTH		FT	COLOUR & SIZE:
CAUGHT		M	RETRIEVE:
LINE			□ MUD □ GRAVEL □ BOULDERS / □ SAND □ ROCKS □ BREAK WALL
		LB	□ WEEDS □ PADS □ BRUSH / □ REEDS □ WEEDLINE □ STUMPS
		KG	□ RAPIDS □ DAM □ ABUTTMENT / □ EDDIES □ SLICK WATER □ HOLDING POOL
LINE TYPE			□ SLOPING □ DROP OFF □ DOCKS / □ FLAT □ HUMP □ OTHER
LOCATION CAUGHT			

PH - A numerical scale from 0 to 14 that is used to express the relative acidity or alkalinity of solutions. The actual value of a given solution is determined by the concentration of hydrogen ions in a solution in which water is a solvent. On the scale, 7 is neutral, values greater than 7 are alkaline and values less than 7 are acidic.

PLANERBOARDING - This is a technique in which special "planerboards" are used along with a lead line and release mechanisms to allow the fisherman to troll his lure out from the sides of his boat rather than behind his boat.

POPPING RODS - This is another name for a Deep Cranking Stick..

POST-SPAWN - The time period right-after spawning when walleye are preparing themselves for their normal seasonal activity.

PRESENTATION - The term used to describe the manner in which you "present" live bait or an artificial lure in front of a fish to make it strike.

Reefs – A chain, mass or ridge of rocks or sand laying at or near the surface of the water.

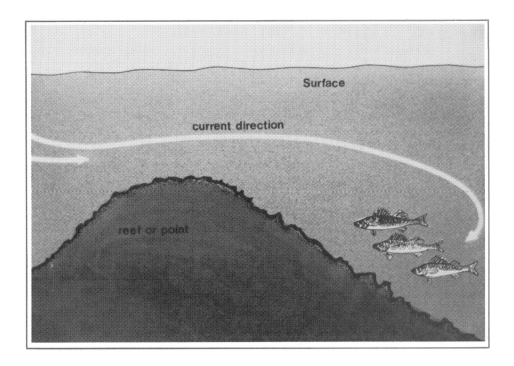

RECOVERY PERIOD – This usually occurs immediately after spawning and at the beginning of the post-spawn period. Many fish species including the walleye require a certain length of time to recover and change from their spawning cycle to their normal seasonal activity.

RIP-JIGGING – This is a jigging technique that is used when fishing very thick weed areas. The angler casts his jig out and allows it to fall to the bottom. When the jig settles, the fisherman snaps the rod back making the jig cut right through aquatic vegetation and then he lets the jig fall to the bottom again. This procedure is repeated over and over again until a fish strikes.

RIVER CHANNEL – This term refers to the "main channel" found in a stream or river. In some cases the river channel is not marked and must be located with the use of a depth finder. In other instances river channels are major navigational paths used by large cargo ships and barges. In many cases river channels are marked and used as "navigational channels".

RIVER SLIPPING – A method used when fishing out of a boat in fast-flowing water. The fisherman keeps the engine running in reverse against the current, this allows the angler to control the boat slower than the normal speed of the current, thus giving him more control over his presentation.

ROCK OUTCROPS – These occur where rock boulders or solid pieces of rock protrude from the bottom to the surface of the water creating a major structure element.

ROD FLEX – This term describes the amount of flexibility that a rod has. Fiberglass rods will be much more flexible than graphite rods.

ROD SENSITIVITY – This term describes how sensitive a rod is when relaying vibrations or movement on the rod tip by the fishing line. Graphite rods will be much more sensitive than fiberglass rods.jd to describe trolling or fishing "strips" that have produced fish in the past.

RUNS – This term designates areas in a river that are created when rapids follow a certain course. This term is also used to describe trolling or fishing "strips" that have produced fish in the past.

"SET" ON A DOWNRIGGER – After attaching the fishing line to the release mechanism on a cannon ball or downrigger cable, the slack line is reeled in until there is a strong bend in the rod. At this point the rod is "set". When a fish triggers the releases, the rod snaps back keeping a tight line on the fish.

SLIDING FLOAT RIGS – A float with a hole through the center is rigged along with a piece of living rubber material above the hook and sinker. The float can run freely up and down the line in between the rubber stopper and the sinkers. The rubber stopper is adjustable and runs through the guides and onto the reel. This makes for easy casting because the float slides to the sinkers. When it hits the water the float allows the line to run through it until it reaches the rubber stopper.

SOUND CHAMBER – A hollow chamber found inside a lure that is usually filled with steel balls that are allowed to roll freely creating a rattling sound.

SNAP – This is a mechanism that is tied to the end of a fisherman's line. It allows the angler to change lures without having to re-tie them each time. Snaps are usually constructed of thin wire material. They can be purchased individually or attached to a swivel.

SNAP-JIGGING – This is another expression for rip-jigging.

SNAP-SWIVEL – This mechanism would be classified as terminal tackle. A snap-swivel is attached to the end of the fishing line and is used to change lures without cutting the line each time.

SPAWN – The stage when fish, amphibians or other aquatic animals deposit their eggs as part of their reproductive cycle.

SPIN-CASTING – This term describes all two-piece rods with pistol grips that are designed to be used with push-button closed faced reels.

SPLASH BOARDS – Panels anchored to the transom of the boat extending ten to fourteen inches up from the transom. These boards are used to deflect water away from the transom of the boat when "back-trolling".

STAINED WATER – Certain types of suspended materials in water can give water a particular colour. In many areas bottom type and water turbulence can create "tea coloured" water. Stained water is usually influenced by the aquatic vegetation growth in a given lake and the type of sediments found on the bottom of the lake.

STILL FISHING – A method of fishing with live bait from a stationary spot either on bottom or suspended without intentionally moving the bait.

STRIKE ZONE – An area located around a fish which is used to attack it's prey. The strike zone will vary in size depending on the fishes activity. In-active fish have a small or non-existing strike zone, feeding fish will have a large strike zone and will move several feet to take a bait.

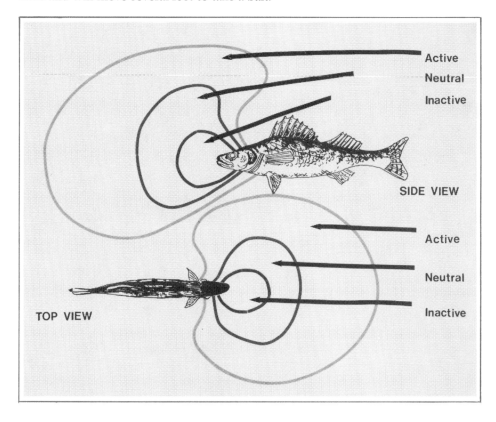

STRUCTURE – A sudden change in bottom depth of five feet or more over a short distance. Such a change is usually created by shorelines, points, islands, rockpiles, bars, reefs, shoals or drop-offs.

SUPRESSION – This is a feature that can be found on various fish finders. The supression control allows the person to suppress short pulses that are being transmitted by the transducer. This feature is desirable when using fish finders at higher then trolling speeds.

SURFACE FEEDERS – A feeding stage of walleye where these fish feed on aquatic organisms, insects and small fish near the surface of a lake.

TAIL-END – This expression is used to describe a section of river or stream that is located immediately after the main pool and just before the next rapids. "Tail-end" of pools are characterized by having slick, flat and fast surface water which turns into rapids.

TAPETUM LUCIDUM – The term used to describe a light sensitive layer of skin that covers the eye of a walleye.

TERMINAL TACKLE – All fishing accessories that are attached to the fishing line which are not lures would be considered terminal tackle. This includes weights, floats, hooks, snaps, snap-swivels and leaders.

THERMOCLINE – A layer of water, found at varying depths, in which the temperature decreases faster than in the layers above and below.

THRUMMING – Some ice-fishing rods have a leaver that allows the angler to "thrum" or shake the line which gives the bait or lure a tantalizing action.

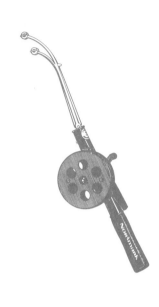

TORQUE – This term describes the amount of pressure that can be exerted with the line and rod when it is applied against a fighting fish.

TRANSDUCER – A crystal transmitting/receiving device that is used with a fish finder. The transducer is that part of a fish finder that is placed below the surface of the water. It sends and receives sound waves in the form of pulses that are recorded by a flasher, liquid crystal or paper recorder.

TRIBUTARY STREAM – Streams feeding larger streams and rivers that eventually flow into a lake.

TURBID – This term describes water that is not clear. Turbidity can be caused from suspended living matter such as algae and plankton or suspended organic sediments and soil.

TWITCHING – A technique used when fishing a wobbling lure on the surface of the water. The fisherman casts the lure out, lets it settle on the surface, then he retrieves using a twitching action.

TWO-PIECE CONSTRUCTION – All fishing rods that can be taken apart in one or more pieces fall under this category.

UNDERWATER POINT – Shoreline points that extend out into deeper water form "underwater points". Most of the time, these major structures can only be located with the use of a fish finder.

UNDRESSED JIG – A jig made up of a jig hook with a molded lead head that is bare. These jigs are usually used with live bait or are "dressed" with hair, bucktail or rubber materials.

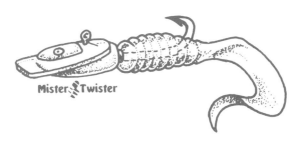

Mister Twister

ULTRALIGHT – Any rod that is very flexible and that is designed to be used with two to four lb. test line and with lures weighing between 1/16 to 1/8 oz. would be classified as "ultralight" in action.

VERTICAL JIGGING – This technique works well when fishing in deeper water. Line is released so that a lure will fall to the bottom. When the lure is suspended near the bottom, the line is drawn tight. The fisherman lifts his rod up lifting the spoon off the bottom, then he lets the spoon "free-fall" back to its bottom position. The depth of the spoon and the length of the "jig lifts" is varied until the fisherman comes up with a productive combination.

VORACIOUS – The term describes a fish that will gorge on anything that will satisfy an excessive appetite.

WALLEYE RIG – A manufactured live bait rig that uses monofilament line and allows the fisherman to use two baits, one above the other suspended under a float or right on the bottom.

WEEDLINE – A weed bed with a defined weed edge constitutes a weedline. Weedlines usually appear as a "wall" of vegetation that meets open water.

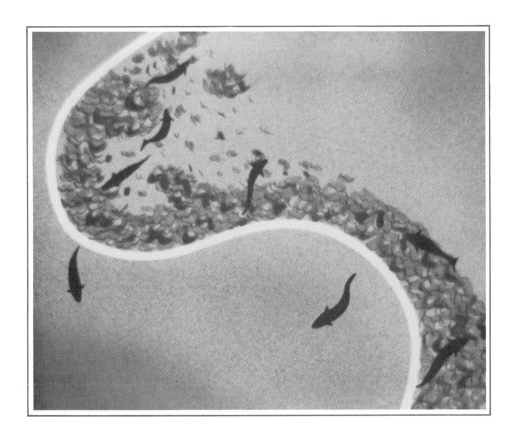

WHITEWATER – An area that is created when fast flowing water goes over obstructions such as rocks and boulders, waterfalls or dams. Whitewater areas are rich in dissolved oxygen and usually indicate shallow "hard pan".

WIRE LEADER – This mechanism would be considered part of terminal tackle. Wire leaders are usually constructed from multi-strand wire coated with a layer of vinyl or plastic. These leaders would be used when fishing for game fish with sharp teeth such as musky and pike.

WOBBLING PLUGS – These lures are constructed of wood, plastic, polyester resin or metal. They are designed to wobble from side to side when they are retrieved. These lures are available in shallow running models to deep diving models.

YOLK SAC – A sac of fatty, protein substance that is part of a newly hatched fish. The yolk sac serves as food for the developing fish.

ZOO PLANKTON – Floating microscopic or near microscopic animals living suspended near the surface of a body of water.

Neutral or Negative Fish

The Artist

Sheilagh Mercer has been the illustrator for Canadian Sportfishing Productions since it's birth. From special assignments like "Canadian Sportfishing (Volume I) – Over 1000 Tips from the Pros", through Logs, video tapes, television art boards to this intricate fishing journal of Walleye Across Canada. Her work can be easily recognized as being nothing short of incredible.

Sheilagh's excellent illustrations describing the written text have helped to make the full line of educational books and video tapes a must for any angler whether they be amateur or pro.

Sheilagh is also an accomplished wood carver and has won a number of classified ribbons in competition. Her artistic achievements are second to none. Even when it comes to special awards, Sheilagh never fails to out do her previous masterpeice. For example, she was recently assigned to carve an exclusive special edition "largemouth bass" for Canadian Sportfishing's sponsor of the year award. This exceptional piece of artwork has become available on special request to the public through Canadian Sportfishing Productions.

1986 recipient ... Berkley of Canada

1987 recipient ... General Motors of Canada

We are very proud to have Sheilagh Mercer as the exclusive artist for Canadian Sportfishing Productions.

Be proud to be a
CANADIAN
SPORTFISHERMAN

Be one of the growing family of successful anglers and educated conservationists.

YOUR MEMBERSHIP IS

When you show proof of purchase (receipt) of one of our **Educational Fishing Tools!**

You can take advantage of the successful techniques Henry and Italo have perfected through the most comprehensive line of Canadian educational fishing products available.

HERE'S WHAT YOU GET

* A personal Membership Card

* A Multi-Coloured Embroidered Canadian Sportfishing Association Patch

* A tough vinyl C.S.A. Decal

* Additional educational information for your 1 year membership term.

Dear Henry and Italo, enclosed please find my proof of purchase of one of your educational fishing tools. I would like to become a **FREE** member of the **Canadian Sportfishing Association.**

PLEASE PRINT

Name _____

Address _____

City_____

Province _____ Zip _____

allow 4-6 weeks delivery

Canada's Greatest

Henry and Italo's series of books, video tapes and fishing tools gives the fisherman, both amateur and pro, professional entertainment and personal tips on exactly where and how to catch their favourite fish. Once you've got the knowledge, their **NEW** POLARIZED FISH'N GLASSES will give you style, eye protection and help you locate fish.

NEW POLARIZED FISH'N GLASSES
Extensive testing, research and development have established our glasses as the best piece of any outdoorsman's equipment. CS-1 sunny days, CS-2 is great for low light and overcast days. Both come with lanyard and case **CS-1, CS-2 $19.95**

CANADIAN SPORTFISHING (VOLUME I)
An illustrated masterpiece of over 1000 fishing tips, hints and techniques on all species **CS-3 $12.95**

WALLEYE ACROSS CANADA (VOLUME II)
An illustrated fishing journal of Walleye Fishing across Canada. This comprehensive book includes every aspect on the subject of Walleye from southern to northern ranges, coast to coast. **CS-4 $14.95**

CANADIAN SPORTFISHING LOG
This log was designed to help you keep an accurate, permanent and resourceful record of your fishing trip for any species, any where **CS-5 $12.95**

CANADIAN SPORTFISHING VIDEO
Two hours of professional fishing entertainment and helpful tips on catching salmon, steelhead, rainbow and speckled trout. **CS-6 $39.95**
Available in VHS & BETA

Educational Tools

Tools For A Proud Canadian Sportfisherman

HAT
CS-7
$8.00
A classic sportfishing hat with our logo. Our hat is made from top grade materials. One size fits all.

PATCH
CS-8
$3.00
A beautiful full coloured embroidered Canadian Sportfishing "Patch of Pride" to show everyone what you stand for.

DECAL
CS-9
$1.00
A colourful Canadian Sportfishing Decal made of tough weather proof vinyl. Use them on vehicles, boats, tackle boxes etc.

PIN
CS-10
$4.00
A colourful lapel pin of our logo. Wear one with pride on your hat, jacket, shirt or sportcoat.

Sport Jackets
CS-11
$69.95
We designed a Sport Jacket to meet the needs of day to day fishing. They cut wind, mist and morning chill, yet can be worn comfortably all day. Handsomely embroidered on the front is our C.S. logo and on the back CANADIAN SPORTFISHING. By the way all jackets are water repellent.

Quantity	Item	Product	Price
_____	C-1	Grey Glasses	19.95
_____	C-2	Amber Glasses	19.95
_____	C-3	VOL I - Tips	12.95
_____	C-4	VOL II - Walleye	14.95
_____	C-5	Log	12.95
_____	C-6	Video ☐ VHS ☐ BETA	39.95
_____	C-7	Hat	7.95
_____	C-8	Patch	3.00
_____	C-9	Decal	1.00
_____	C-10	Pin	4.00
_____	C-11	Jacket	69.95

Mens S (36-38)   M (38-40)   L (40-42)   XL (44-46)
Method of Payment (check one)
☐ CHECK   ☐ MONEY ORDER   ☐ VISA

Visa # _____

Card Exp. _____ Signature _____

Name _____

Address _____

City _____

Province _____ Postal _____

Canadian Sportfishing Productions
P.O. Box 84, Carlisle, Ontario L0R 1H0

Acknowledgements

Photos, Artwork and Sponsors

- Alexander Doug
- B&B Typesetting
- Berkley Ltd.
- Canadian Pacific
- Canadian Coleman
- Canadian Sportfishing Productions
- Duracell Canada
- Esso
- General Motors of Canada
- Hayakawa Mike
- Hills Video Productions
- Honda
- Kerr Brian
- Kettle Creek Canvas Co.
- Labatt
- Lake Systems Division
- Lowrance Electronics
- Lure King
- McCord Rick
- McDonald Charlie
- Mercer Sheilagh
- Mister Twister
- Mustang Industries
- Normark Industries
- Northland
- Ontario Federation of Anglers and Hunters
- Outdoor Canada Magazine
- Outboard Marine Corporation
- Peterborough Boats
- Peter Storm
- Plano
- Smith Dave
- Skeeter Boats
- Williams